ONE THING ONLY

ONE THING ONLY

A Christian Guide to the Universal
Quest for God

by
Lois Lang-Sims

A NEW ERA BOOK

Paragon House
New York

To Father Francis
in Gratitude

First edition, 1988

Published by
Paragon House
90 Fifth Avenue
New York, NY 10011

Library of Congress Cataloging-in-Publication Data

Lang-Sims, Lois.
  One thing only.

  1. Christian life–1960–   2. Knowledge,
Theory of (Religion)   I. Title.
BV4501.2.L31842 1988   230   88-6007
ISBN 0-913757-92-6

Manufactured in the United States of America

Contents

Introduction

This book is an attempt to lead the reader on the Way of Truth. Its author has no qualifications for leading anyone save one: she knows how that Way is to be found. It is to be found in the essential teachings that have come down to us through the great religious traditions. It is to be found in the testimony of the true mystics of those same traditions, whose knowledge, acquired in humility, transcends all apparent differences between the various systems of ritual, symbolism, and myth. It is to be found, above all, insofar as we pay attention to the inner voice that speaks with certainty within the heart. In finding and following this Way, we shall learn that the ground beneath our feet is our everyday life. But we will not understand the circumstances of our lives, and we shall never deal with them properly, until we are able to see them in the light of Truth.

In studying the great traditions, we have to begin with our own. It is our own tradition, whether this be Christianity, Islam, Judaism, Hinduism, Buddhism, or any

other that has been validated down the ages by the witness
of its sages and saints, that has formed those structural
patterns in our minds that respond to its symbolism, as one
dances in a certain way to a certain kind of music, and
no other way will do. In this book we start out from the
Christian tradition, and stay with it in the sense that we
turn our gaze upon the riches of the other great religions
from its point of view, always in the knowledge that all
the forms and formulas must come together at that point
which is the truth of certainty within the human heart.
That point is the End of the Quest. There we find the
Reality of Realities (to use an Islamic phrase). So the End
is the Beginning since we must start from it and return to
it. That is what the mystics did, and continue to do; and
we need to make a study of their writings or at least of
a selection of them. (It is not good to read either too little
or too much.)

Our own times are unique in that the entire system
of values that characterizes them is squarely in opposition
to the essential message of religious tradition, which is
always and everywhere the same: the purpose of our lives,
our societies, our world, is One Thing Only – to return,
as swiftly and surely as we can, to God. Every word that
we utter, every action that we undertake, every secondary
aim that we pursue, is harmful to us insofar as it is not
harnessed to this purpose. It is to redirect the minds of its
readers to this purpose that this book has been written.
It should be read simply as an indication of where and how
to begin.

Metaphysical truth is not communicable by means of
a linear argument. In the metaphysical realm every
statement made is related to every other one in such a way
that each follows from each, and the seeker is perpetually
going off on a tangent and coming back. It is necessary
to still the logical processes of the rational mind, allowing

the spiritual eye to open and wander, as a spotlight wanders, here and there among the images of truth. Together these images make up a consistent whole that one must try to see, a mandala or picture-pattern, with certain key motifs arranged in such a way that the eye is led to return to them again and again until it becomes impossible to see any part of the pattern except in relationship to its central point. So in this book it has not been possible to arrange the material in a logical sequence, or to avoid repetition wherever it becomes necessary to emphasize some vital link.

As the Quest proceeds, it is necessary to understand how to combine urgency with patience. *Festina lente* ("hasten slowly") was a maxim much cherished by the philosophers and artists of the neoplatonism of the Renaissance, who used it to reinforce the idea that one cannot fully understand anything until one has seen it in its proper relationship to every other thing. This, one would suppose, takes a long time! On the other hand, insofar as one is able to gaze steadily at the center, it can happen at once. Patience is demanded because this act of concentration is something given rather than achieved by one's efforts (although those efforts must be made), and because it is folly to decide that because a certain proposition appears at first sight to be unacceptable, it will not be clarified in the light of further ideas as these unfold themselves gradually in relationship to it.

When this book has been read and pondered over, what then? The author refrains deliberately from detailed recommendations of practices to be followed or books to be obtained. The first necessity for the seeker is to seek. Go first to the great ones: Julian, Rumi (whose writings transcend all distinctions between Muslim and Christian), the *Philokalia*; the list is endless, but one should not, therefore, permit one's own use of it to be the same! Limitation is an absolute necessity of the spiritual life. One should find and cherish what is providentially intended for oneself. As for the vast mountain of reading material that is nowadays being presented to us with the avowed object of directing us along the path of Truth, it is tempting to suggest that the seeker should unhesitatingly let it alone. But this is not really possible or even desirable. The individual, guided by those basic principles he has already gleaned from more reliable works, must find his own way amid all this advice and information. In doing so he will make mistakes; it is even necessary that he should. For the young in particular, it is rightly inevitable that they should face the philosophical and moral problems that will beseige them as they take their place in contemporary society. They may study various aspects of these problems in the works of contemporary thinkers, including, of course, psychologists and scientists. The only suggestion that one dares to make is that nothing should be read or investigated unless there appears to be a real possibility that it will help answer some important question or remove some troublesome impediment. To smother oneself under a load of literature on meditation, mysticism, occultism, cosmology, and related matters is positively harmful; to confine oneself to detective fiction and simple prayers is not, though it may not be all that one should be doing at a given moment. There is a time for all things, including books. And curiously, the more one becomes capable of reading anything that happens to be available without bewilderment and loss of faith, the less one is inclined to read anything but that tiny selection from the works of the great masters that one knows to be one's own essential nourishment.

The one sure guide through the labyrinth is prayer. "Let me follow the intimations of the will of God," said Socrates on the way to his death. That is prayer. And we are all of us on the way to our deaths. That way will turn out to be the Way. It leads us to the One Thing Only, which will not be recognized until we are prepared to believe, and seek finally to know, that nothing else is of the slightest importance, to you, to me, to anyone, or anything upon this planet earth or anywhere else in time and space.

Festina lente.

Blessed be God.

1

Where Shall We Begin?

"Let each one of us leave every other kind of knowledge, and seek and follow one thing only." In *The Republic* Plato sums up in these words the message of every saint and sage our world has known or will ever know. They are words intended for us all, hard, uncompromising words. They speak of something that is Simplicity itself; but we, because we are not simple, must approach that essential Simplicity by a variety of complex means embracing every sphere of human life. These means unfold themselves slowly within a tradition. A great religious tradition is consistent in all its parts, an integrated manifestation of that which transcends manifestation, Plato's "one thing only," for which we use the code word *God*.

For the individual brought up within the context of a revealed religion (one, that is to say, that began with, and continues by means of, an influx of spiritual power and enlightenment) accepted and practiced by an integrated community, insofar as the will is present the means to "seek and follow" are at hand. Nowadays few, if any, of us are in this auspicious situation. A kind of spiritual promiscuity defeats our ends. The great traditons are becoming increasingly entangled one with another, in such a way that the living Spirit has no coherent form within which to flow and do its work, at the same time as they are being "reformed" from within to meet a diversity of human requirements with which, in reality, they have little or nothing to do. Outside the Communist-dominated countries, which present their own difficulties, at least as grave but to some extent distinguishable from those to be encountered elsewhere, this situation is worldwide. Where it exists, unadmitted delusion comes into its own. In a world where it is becoming all but impossible to follow the Platonic exhortation within the context of what is left of any one of the major religions, the "devout" are often self-deceivers, clinging to decaying structures and unreal "beliefs," while the self-styled "unbeliever" may well be a sincere, if bitterly frustrated, seeker after truth.

Robert Herrick, whose poetry has the quality of pure simplicity, reminds us in one of his poems, "Truth by her own simplicity is known"; and we recognize that this is so, but find that what should be the easiest thing in the world is, in practice, the most difficult. We return to the basic simplicities only insofar as we are prepared to "leave aside every other kind of knowledge" and remain open only to what is relevant to the end being sought. Everything in our world that is real can, if we so choose, and if it is right for us at the time, be related to that end. All the beauty and all the pain can, if we so choose, be made transparent to God: only the trivial, the senseless and the for-us inappropriate (which is harder to accept) will impede us; only these are a waste of time. But still we need help. We do not easily discriminate between the true and the false; still less between what we really need at any given moment and what we had better do without. Our minds are fevered and bursting with too much information, too many answers, too many books.

The great traditions may be, in one sense, in decline; but in another they remain available to us, if we learn to make our own the wisdom contained in their scriptures and the writings of their saints. This is not to be done by promiscuous reading, but by a slow process of deep assimilation, and by seeking out the places and the people whose influence is likely to be substantial and permanent. Slowly the mind becomes angled to a certain fundamental point of view, and to those ideas which may properly be called "religious" as opposed to the assumptions of a secular humanism. The several religious traditions must never be confused: we should not attempt to synthesize them (any more than we should divide them into categories such as "monotheistic" or "dualistic" or transpose their symbols and mythologies one upon another, making equivalencies that are often tempting but seldom exact. On the other hand, because these traditions spring initially from one center and lead infallibly to one End (that Center and that End being one and the same), they have in common certain fundamental beliefs concerning our world and human life. They tell us the same things about our origin and about our end. They point out what is necessary and what is not; and this is the same for every one of us as we travel between birth and death. Each of them contains within itself the possibility of them all; therefore, no one of them is "heresy" in relationship to another; they are but differing formulations of a single Truth. Truth in its pristine simplicity is approachable from an infinite number of paths diverging from and again converging towards a single point. Properly understood, "heresy" is the rejection of what leads us to the "one thing" in favor of that which turns us back upon ourselves—our pride, our laziness, our lusts. Any image, any pattern of behavior, that is metaphyscially false, and so tends towards a false judgment of the human situation, is heresy in the sense originally given to that word by the Fathers of the Church, before it became trivialized and abused to mean anything that was outwardly at variance with the exoteric dogmas imposed by Rome. It is metaphysical error that misleads, and it does so right down the scale from the highest flights of the questing mind to the humblest practical details of everyday life.

We cannot all be metaphysicians. But most of us are capable of meditating upon the written testimonies and the works of art arising out of the revelation to mankind, within the great traditions, of the basic metaphysical structure of reality that shapes our lives. This we are bound to do; although we must do it nowadays with little or no assistance from religious institutions, which are more likely to confuse our minds than to clarify for us their own inheritance. In the past every child was born into this world within the context of a living faith. Certain prescribed patterns were built into his way of life. The metaphysical truths in accordance with which those patterns had been structured were made known to him in terms of ritual formulas and sacred myths. If, as he grew older, he desired to study and learn by degrees to understand the interiorities of his religion, he could do so; indeed, for those who have an aptitude for the higher knowledge, it is a sin to neglect its pursuit. In general, however, for one born into a viable tradition there is no pressing need, in the absence of an exceptional vocation, to know more than that the forms of that tradition, lovingly and steadfastly obeyed for the sake of the Spirit present in those forms, point out the path that leads to everlasting joy and peace in God. For such a one, the necessity of seeking and following "one thing only" cannot be in doubt. Tradition makes itself plain: failure is one thing; uncertainty about the goal and the way to achieve it is something else. We, who are no worse if not better than our forefathers, are born into uncertainty. The child of our time, unless he has the quality of simplicity to a degree found only in the saints, is likely to remain in that state unless he is able and willing to learn how to study and discriminate. A proliferation of information and opinions is being forced upon him from morning till night. His task is not so much to sift through all this dreary mind-stuff, as to turn away from it to surer sources of enlightenment.

Metaphysical truth is expressed in man, in his bodily form and the activities proper to his nature, as well as in the order and beauty of his natural environment where this is permitted to remain unspoiled; but the knowledge of it is communicated by means of sacred rituals, mythologies and works of art. These constitute a kind of distillation or concentration of the eternal verities into forms that have been sacralized, as it is believed, by virtue of having been returned by and from nature to God to become the vehicles of enlightenment. Sacred geometry—which provides, for example, a diagram of the Trinity, an idea central to Christian theology—was used by our forefathers to plot the relationships at the heart of reality, and became the basis for the visual arts, of which the architecture of the temple was both the highest expression and the focal point. In the world of sound, the laws of harmony were put to the same essential use; similarly, in the case of the spoken and written word, measurement and proportion governed the formal presentation of metaphysical truths, whether as poetry, liturgy or doctrinal statement. Behind all this, perhaps the clearest and most popularly effectual of all the various means of religious communication was the sacred myth.

A sacred myth is a story, each succeeding episode of which unfolds from its central theme to express, in terms of interrelated images, the motions of Divinity within itself and within and toward mankind. Thus in the Christian myth, the birth of Christ, his Passion and Resurrection, his return to heaven and the crowning of his Mother as the Bride of God, depict the Mysteries of our origin and end and of the soul's rebirth. At the same time, because of the correspondences that appear in a world where every level reflects in its own way the one above, this same myth can be transposed into astrological, alchemical, psychological, and physical terms, always with the understanding that its "explanation" is not reducible to those terms. In fact, it can never be adequately explained. A sacred myth is its own explanation. We are required to participate in it until we ourselves become identified with the meaning it communicates. What we must not do is to confuse mythological episodes with historical events. The post-Renaissance West developed a concept of history that was not shared by those who came before, and is by no means universal even now. We have been conditioned to perceive history as a line of "real" events that "happened" in a physically substantial and objective sense that even our own science has recently called into dispute. Yet at the same time as we ascribe to history the kind of reality which it does not and cannot possess — *cannot*, because our "seeming" world is but a partial, and to some extent distorted, version of what really is — we deny to the line of time along which we presently move the possibility of a continued existence. We relegate it to an unreal past. It *was*, we say, and now it *is not.* These confusions make it impossible for us to understand the nonhistorical reality of myth. The Christian Church has felt obliged to ascribe what we think of as "historical reality" to mythological events. In doing so, it has bestowed divine status upon one who claimed no such thing for himself. (This was so, of course, from the beginning: it is not in itself a post-Renaissance phenomenon. The point to be remembered is that earlier notions of "history" were such that what our forefathers believed in was, in fact, the reality of their myths. This is the exact opposite of our own position, whether we realize it or not.) Islam, without claiming actual divinity for the Prophet, has followed the same principle in many respects. All this is deeply misleading. Gautama Buddha, Jesus of Nazareth, and Muhammad were indeed the temporary representatives upon earth of archetypal beings who exist beyond time and whose eternal relationships even an inspired mythology cannot adequately express, but their individual personalities were unimportant compared with the roles they undertook. Their personal identities were submerged in a willed identification with the Mysteries for the sake of which they lived and died. Every one of us will be called upon eventually to do even as they did. The Perfect Man, the Enlightened One, the Christ: these beings are more, far more, than Gautama Buddha or Muhammad or Jesus. The truth of the myths does not depend upon what "happened" in historic time. If those of us who are Christians had even the most elementary understanding of the nature of time, we should not be worrying about the historical evidence for the entry into it of the Son of God.

In fact, it becomes necessary entirely to rearrange our thoughts about time; and this is far from being the only mental rearrangement that we have to make. To enter the realms of metaphysical studies is to realize almost at once that the rules of logic to which we have become accustomed have ceased to be appropriate. No longer is it possible to proceed with a logical argument step by step. The word *because* retires into the background. And an unforeseen difficulty arises: it becomes impossible to understand any one idea without reference to so many others, many of which will not already have been explained, that one is forever going off on a tangent, glancing in some new direction and then coming back, only to return later to

a fuller consideration of what previously was only glimpsed.
Metaphysical truth is a simple unity: therefore, however
many times it is broken up into its own aspects, it can never
be represented as a chain of propositions proceeding in a
linear sequence. In order to explain, for instance, the story
of the Annunciation to the Virgin of the birth of Christ,
it will be necessary to initiate the inquirer—gradually, of
course, and in accordance with the capacity of his
understanding—into the entire mythological and doctrinal
system of the Christian religion; and, in fact, in a traditional
society this is how religious instruction would normally
proceed. In such a society, the question asked would not
anticipate an isolated explanation, but a placing of the
subject of inquiry carefully within a framework already
partially understood. In a mythological story, the apparently
sequential events unfold out of and into one another in
such a way that the Annunciation to Mary is not only a
cause *of* but is caused *by* the Resurrection of her Son. The
two episodes imply, contain, and reflect one another, two
pictures of, or ways of looking at, the central act which
is the inner meaning of the myth.

We are presently in a strange predicament. Our world
has become meaningless to us, for the reason that we are
unable to assess and understand not only "religious" ideas
but (since all truths are interdependent) any idea whatsoever
in a context from which the principle of wholeness has been
unobtrusively removed. This situation will continue until
we can re-establish a point of view from which it is possible
to place every new idea in relationship to others within
an ordered system corresponding to the unity of Truth.
"For all things that exist are seen to be ordered to each
other," as Aquinas said. The idea of the elephant's trunk
is not to be comprehended apart from the idea of the
elephant. In a traditional society the "elephant" is apprehended gradually; in its wholeness at the same time as the

"trunk." If we cannot any longer achieve this simple, unfragmented point of view, how shall we find it again? We are not in the position of the blind man feeling only a trunk or a foot without ever having had a notion of the entire animal. Even our excess of miscellaneous information is a disadvantage to us. The saints and sages of the great religions were no more obliged than were the common folk to ask themselves questions about the historicity or the scientific feasibility of their myths. Their education, based upon a central assumption from which a scheme of knowledge extended in concentric circles towards an undefined circumference that was limited in each case by the real capacities and vocation of the recipient, did not raise irrelevant questions in their minds. Nowadays none of us is able to avoid such questions, even when (which is rare) we have come to understand their unimportance. We have to extricate ourselves from habits of mind that were formed by a type of "education" that is both misdirected and far too wide-ranging for any but the strongest and most steadily orientated mental faculties to assimilate. Our dilemma is, by this time, unavoidable. It means simply that we must exercise a degree of patience even greater and more humble than that which would once have been required in the early stages of the Quest.

2

How and What
Do We Know?

The first question to be asked is whether there is anything that, initially, we *know*. For if, initially, we know nothing, we never can know anything.

It is necessary to make sure from the outset that we are not to be the victims of a circular argument. "Because the Bible tells me so" (which, despite its obvious absurdity, was the chorus of a once popular hymn) is one such argument. Substitute "my reason" or "my insights" for "the Bible" and we have two others; there are many more. Since no initial proposition can be proved, one may ask how to escape the trap. But that for which "every other kind of knowledge" must be left behind is present in the heart before the search for and the following of the "One Thing Only" is undertaken by the questing soul. It is both the End and the Beginning of the Quest.

We cannot begin without some degree of faith, although it be all but imperceptible. What is faith? It is not, as is sometimes erroneously supposed, the same thing as belief in the sense that I "believe" that Rome is in Italy and that I am sitting at this table in this house. What is "Rome," what is "Italy," and who am "I"? We may imagine that our beliefs, or at least some of them, are absolute; but they never can be anything of the sort. In any case they belong to a category which, in this matter, is beside the point. Faith is reasonable, but it is not based upon reason. The so-called "proofs" of God so dear to medieval theologians were put forward to demonstrate its reasonableness, not to suggest that we could, or had any need to, start out from them. They are not enough.

"Faith is the substance of things hoped for, the evidence of things not seen," St. Paul wrote in one of his letters to the Hebrews. This verse suggests that our faith is itself the evidence for its own object and that it is in some way to be substantially identified with that object. (Again we find the idea that subject and object, beginning and end, are never wholly separate, and will ultimately be joined together in a realized unity that will then be seen to have existed all the time.)

The tenth-century Sufi mystic Muhammad b. Khafif expressed this concept as nearly perfectly as words can when he wrote, "Faith is the belief of the heart in that knowledge which comes from the unseen." We are required, then, to believe in a knowledge. The knowledge is something given. It comes to us and is not dependent upon "proofs" but is its own evidence. The anonymous mystic who was known to the medieval Church as Dionysius the Areopagite and was confused with St. Paul's Athenian convert (although in fact he lived several centuries later and was a Christian Neoplatonist, teaching probably in Alexandria) defines this knowledge as "the look which goes from God into the soul." He calls this look "the beginning of faith."

Faith begins in what seems at first to be total darkness. At the heart of the darkness is a point of light, just as the picture on a television screen vanishes inwards to a point.

Here, unlike the dead screen, there is always the living possibility at the center of what we call the self. Julian of Norwich, the fourteenth-century anchorite whose metaphysical genius is nowadays all too frequently sentimentalized, tells us in her *Revelations* that she "saw God in a Point, that is to say in mine understanding—by which sight I saw that he is in all things." The Sufis call this point the Eye of Certainty, the organ of spiritual sight which is the implantation of Divinity by Divinity, whereby It knows Itself. The Sufis have a sacred chant which includes these words:

> Open the eye of thy heart so that thou wilt see the Spirit
> So that thou wilt see that which cannot be seen.

That faculty in man which functions by means of the spiritual eye to perceive divine things is frequently referred to in English mystical literature as the intellect, to be distinguished carefully from the rational faculty, which serves the intellect up to a certain point and then becomes redundant. Nowadays, this usage results in confusion, modern man having chosen to identify his intellect with his reasoning powers, recognizing nothing beyond. In Latin, however, *intellectus* means "understanding," and true understanding can be achieved only when we have learned to recognize and use the organ of enlightenment situated in the place of the heart. The heart, not the head, is the seat of Divinity within; not, of course, the merely physical heart, but its invisible counterpart, mainspring of the living Spirit. Mental confusion is inevitably accompanied in a vicious circle by verbal misuse. An example of this is the positively avid appropriation by contemporary theologians and popular writers on religion of the word *insight* to describe anything and everything from the revelations accorded to the saints and sages of the past to their own bright ideas in the present. This word represents a reaction against the previous overemphasis on rationality by those who are incapable of transcending rationality but can only oppose it with an equally disastrous mistake. Worse still, it is a product of the horizontalism that is the rampant heresy of our times. Used correctly, it refers to the psychical level of our being and is indispensable to the language. Scattered indiscriminately on almost every page of almost every new book to be found in a "religious" bookshop, it denotes a point of view that excludes deliberately the concept of an inwardly revealed knowledge in favor of an intuitive exercise initiated by oneself. Anyone who supposes that, unaided by Divine grace, he is capable of "seeing into" the realities of the human state, let alone those greater Realities that contain, surround, and bestow meaning upon that state, has rejected the knowledge of the heart which is perceived by the intellectual faculty and comes from God. The great mystics would not thank us for congratulating them on their "insights."

No one perceives darkness who knows nothing of the light. Still it remains true that a great many people are inclined to protest that they do indeed see only darkness; they are unaware of, and disinclined to believe in, that Eye of Certainty which, for most of us, has barely opened yet. Thus the cultivation of "insights" is no way of learning how to see. The true way is more humble: it consists in the practice of religion (by means of private prayer and, where they continue to be available in a viable form, participation in the rites); the pursuit of justice, which is the beginning of love; true repentance for one's sins; and the study of traditonal wisdom in the writings of the saints. Psychical experiences, even when good in themselves, are generally inimical to the faculty of direct vision. This faculty is operative at a level which is, mysteriously, both above and (in the sense of being at a more profound depth than) below the field of psychical, emotional, and personal agitation; and a great deal of preparation is needed before we are able to recognize and use it as it is intended to be used. In the spiritual life, to suppose that we receive something for nothing may be true in the sense that we deserve nothing, but it is far from true regarding the work that must be done.

We labor under grievous disadvantages of course. In a normal society, based upon an initial revelation and orientated towards a divinely appointed End, every individual would benefit directly from the wisdom bestowed upon a few, and every individual would be given the opportunity to become, by dedication, study, and self-sacrifice, one of those few. Whether there has ever been a society that could claim to be fully and operatively "normal" in this sense may be open to question. What is beyond dispute is that never before in human history has mankind rejected the ideal and the intention to bring it about—never before until now, when the forms that once regulated our lives are being torn apart, and nothing but the most outrageous abnormalities accepted in their place.

We are entitled to assume that the primary revelation, made at a period of time now lost beneath upheavals that obliterated all traces of its recipients, was of a relatively simple character and a blinding purity, and that it contained by implication all that was to come.[1] From this initial communication there would have arisen, as mankind dispersed itself, the various traditions, in accordance with the particular needs and capacities of the several collectivities that settled in different parts of the world. These traditions were the providential means whereby humanity was to be returned. They provided both an inner (esoteric) knowledge and the outer framework of a way of life. According to the Quranic verse:

We shall show them our signs upon the horizons and
within their souls until it becomes manifest to them that
it is the Truth.

This showing of "signs" by God can never have been
anything other than a direct communication to the human
heart; so that if we think of it as having been made
originally, or at any other time, to a group, we are falling
into a grave mistake. Henry Corbin, who is considered to
be one of the outstanding exponents of Sufi mysticism at
the present time, makes this point with remarkable clarity
in his book *The Man of Light in Iranian Sufism*: "essentially
what has just been referred to as 'superconsciousness' . . .
cannot be a collective phenomenon. It is always something
that opens up at the end of a struggle in which the
protagonist is the spiritual individuality . . . Without doubt
a mystical fraternity will result from it, but does not exist
before it."

It is important to stress this understanding at the present
time and within a Christian context. Within the Churches[2]
today it is fashionable to decry the individual experience,
even to the extent of advocating something miscalled "group
contemplation" and stressing the supposed superiority of
a concelebrated Mass over one that is celebrated by a single
officiating priest. We need to find, analyze, and hold onto
a clear distinction between the "group" as a concept arising
out of the modern idea of "community" on a social and
personal level, and the idea of the Mystical Church.
Community is a word that acquires its true meaning and
value only when seen as deriving from the "mystical
fraternity" which has come into being as the result rather
than the condition of an individual experience. The
Anglican theologian Charles Williams made a remarkable
contribution to the English language when he wrote of the

unity-in-diversity of blessed souls as the "Co-inherence."
Within the Co-inherence (which is the Church in its true
meaning, beyond that of any earthly institution) each
individual soul is alone with God; and yet, since God is
all, reunion with Him implies reunion with "all that shall
be saved," as Julian puts it again and again (and Julian clearly
believed that none would be excluded at the end of time).
In the final consummation each is in all and all in each:
that is the cause and meaning of the commandment that
we should love one another; it obliges us to join together
in worship, to pursue justice and cooperate in all that we
do, but not at the cost of denying the direct, uninterrupted
intercourse between the soul and God as being the origin
of grace.

It is significant that the word *grace*, with all its
connotations of a descending gift, has in recent times been
virtually ousted from the theological vocabulary of the
Christian Church. Its liturgical usage carries three meanings:
revelation, or the communication of knowledge; purification
and reconciliation, without which spiritual progress is
impossible; and the strength required to conform oneself
to the will of God. A great deal of confusion has arisen
through a misunderstanding of the story of the descent of
grace in the person of the Holy Spirit upon the twelve
disciples in the Upper Room. This story, which is both
historical, as a description of a particular outpouring at the
initiation of a tradition, and mythical, as an image of the
totality of God's action towards the world, describes
something that is essentially an individual experience,
although it involves individuals gathered together in a group
and bonded together by the love of God. It should not
be forgotten that Pentecost represents an aspect of the
Eucharistic rite: it is, as it were, the response of the Spirit
to Christ's sacrificial act. Jesus, invisibly present, is the central
figure, the officiating priest. Through Him, as He rises to

heaven,[3] the descending Spirit falls upon the twelve, in its totality upon each one; there can never be a division of the indivisible gift of grace, as there can never be a division of God's giving of Himself to each and every opened heart.

If all this seems like an unnecessary splitting of hairs, it is not so; because, in fact, it involves the distinction between the "mystical fraternity," brought into being as an effect of the communion of each one of its members with the One, and at the opposite extreme the amorphous "masses" of the Communist and humanist mystique. (That humanism leads to Communism by an inexorable logic only their own illogicality enables humanists to deny. Only Communism and the various forms of Fascism present logical alternatives to the sacred traditions.) According to that mystique, the welded-together majority represents the source of all power and all judgment. Ultimately it is a question of whether humanity itself is to be regarded as its own divinity without reference to anything above itself; and that is precisely the sin recommended in the book of Genesis by the serpent: "Ye shall be as gods." If grace is to descend upon us from above, it can do so only by establishing a one-to-One communion which expands in love by virtue of the love of God. In loving God I love all creatures that were made by Him; but I can love God only insofar as I receive His love into the innermost recesses of my heart, in a secret exchange whereby He permits me to love Him with His own love, because He has taken my place within me.

The great world teachers, founders of the sacred traditions, were those to whom was entrusted a particular kind of communication providentially intended for the direction of the destiny of mankind. It has been said that these exceptional beings came down from heaven, having completed their earthly pilgrimage and chosen to return, solely for the purpose of reclaiming their fellow beings by their teaching, example, and self-sacrifice. On the other hand, there are hints of a convergence between a fully evolved human being and this mystical descent. The matter has seldom if ever been made explicit, perhaps because it is beyond our human comprehension here on earth. Jalalu'l-Din Rumi, thirteenth-century Sufi poet and saint, wrote of the Pirs, who, as heads of the orders of dervishes, are assumed to have achieved enlightenment:

> The Pirs are they whose spirits were in the sea of the
> Divine Munificence before this world existed.
> They lived ages before the creation of the body; they
> harvested the wheat before it was sown.
> Before the form was molded, they had received the spirit;
> before the sea was made, they had strung the pearl.

How could it be otherwise? Basic to all the great traditions is the idea that the greater comes before the lesser; that which is nearer to God is prior to that which is farther off. So all reductionism is antitraditional and foolish. The song of a bird is its praise of God; the fact that it has a territorial explanation, on the merely physical level, in no way affects the priority of its essential function: it is that function which causes it to be. In accordance with the same principle, Muslims declare that it was for the sake of "the Reality of Muhammad" (a strange phrase, seeming to imply that the historical figure was but a partial manifestation at a particular time and place of a pre-existent Reality transcending place and time) that God created the world.

The story of the communication of the Qur'an to Muhammad closely parallels that of the Annunciation to the Virgin of the birth of Christ. The two stories represent the opening mythological images of their respective traditions: they describe the entry into creation of the Word of Truth. Muhammad inquires of the archangel how he can fulfill the command to write at the angelical dictation, seeing that he is illiterate. Mary asks how she can conceive a child when she has had no intercourse with a man. In both cases, question and answer have the same meaning. Nothing but the heart that is empty of all else can be filled with the Spirit and conceive the Word. The Holy Babe and the Holy Book are images of revelation. There is a parallel between the man Jesus and the actuality of the Qur'an in the sense that both are of an altogether extraordinary character by virtue of the Mystery they represent; yet they are not in themselves that Mystery; other manifestations of a similarly tremendous significance may take place. The Buddha declared of Himself: "I am the Holy One in this world, I am the highest teacher, I alone am the Absolute Sambuddha . . ." There is no opposition between this "claim" and those of Jesus. Neither refers to the personal self, lost in a selfless identification with "the Man of Light."

Such, then are the beginnings from which a tradition opens out. Vehicle of grace and of revelation, it develops from the simplicity of its initial formulation into an ever-increasing complexity, from which it draws back into simplicity once again in the experience of its saints. At its root is that Truth which "by her own simplicity is known." It is in order to protect that very simplicity that it becomes necessary to elaborate it. For instance, the purpose of the immensely complex mythology of Hinduism and the intricately structured liturgies of the Catholic Church is the purveyance of the spiritual benefits of tradition to those of us who are not yet capable of direct vision. It is by such means that a collectivity is ordered, in conformity with a primary revelation, and it is not only societies that constitute collectivities; every individual human being is in himself a more or less orderly system of potentially conflicting elements destined eventually to be reunited by the Word of Truth. So we have the first stage of elaboration consisting in the production of sublime mythologies, rituals, and sacraments. From these arise symbolic works of art, followed by the development of doctrine, a phenomenon particularly in evidence, for various historic reasons, in the Roman Catholic Church.

The enormously complicated doctrinal system evolved over the centuries by Rome eventually defeated its own ends by provoking the violent reactions that followed the initial relaxation of its rigidities by Vatican II. But rigidity and its outcome in reaction are not the inevitable results of even the most hair-splitting formulations of doctrine; they are the outcome of a state of fear on the part of human beings who have begun to be attached to their own power. A doctrine is formulated, in the first instance, with the negative but wholly justifiable object of protecting, by means of a verbal definition, a truth that is in danger of being distorted or lost. A doctrinal system has an intellectual beauty of its own, provided it remains living and flexible, without demanding a too literal and legalistic acceptance of the formulations it presents. One must learn to distinguish between the metaphysical reality which is the essential basis of a given formulation, and the literal interpretation, which must never be allowed to harden into a dogmatic statement hedged about with threats. The tragedy of the Roman Catholic Church in the upheavals following Vatican II lay in the inability of its hierarchy to make this distinction. Never before have so many precious truths been rejected because the doctrines in which they had been encapsulated, having been interpreted in an exclusively literal and historical sense, appeared to have become obsolete.

Yet this need not have been so. An experience of vision-in-humility could have directed the Church toward the rediscovery of its own esotericism. The hard shell of solidified doctrine could, beneath the gentle flame of the

Spirit, have been melted away to reveal the treasure trove beneath. And even now, for the true seeker, this great exercise of rediscovery can be undertaken individually, within the co-inherence of the Mystical Church. One can still read. One can study the scriptures, the old liturgies, the lives and testimonies of the saints, until the underlying *gnosis* is revealed, in the light of which no further difficulty will be experienced. I am not suggesting that no reform of wording and presentation was required. What was absolutely not required was the thoughtless rejection of even a single word without recalling what it really meant.

All of us are born of, if not any longer into, a tradition. This may not be true for more than another generation; but it remains sufficiently so today for those of us who are natives of the Western world to have the imprint of Christianity upon the very mind-stuff that enables us to think. A great many people have reacted against this inescapable condition. Choosing to regard the exterior blemishes of their own tradition rather than its metaphysical content, and to do the reverse with regard to other and less familiar faiths, they have fallen victim to all manner of confusions. To attempt to identify oneself with an alien religion, no matter how sublime its tenets and its symbolism, without having properly examined one's own, is liable to mean that one loses a reality and is left with an illusion. Why should we not drink of the river that has watered our own fields? But let us never lose sight of the transcendental unity[4] of all those religions for which the primeval revelation was the common source. At the highest pinnacle of vision, the formulations are abandoned like vehicles no longer in use. So Rumi cries out:

> Lo, for I to myself am unknown, now in God's name what must I do?
> I adore not the Cross nor the Crescent, I am not a

Giaour nor a Jew.
East nor West, land nor sea is my home...
In a place beyond uttermost place, in a tract without
shadow or trace,
Soul and body transcending I live in the Soul of my
Loved One anew!

We have returned here to the simplicity and the silence.
But we have to follow the path of complexity in order to
arrive at this state.

3

Can We Know God?

We begin with a paradox. We, of ourselves, can know nothing. Yet it is given us to know all that we need to know, as we grow into the capacity for knowledge. God knows in us and for us. He knows Himself in us; and there is nothing to be known that is other than God. Muhammad ascribes to Him these words: "I was a Hidden Treasure; and I desired to be known..."

Muslims have found the explanation of creation in this statement. God knows Himself in His creation, and the place of that knowing is the heart of man. No man can, of himself, know God. Yet, since God has willed to know Himself in us, we can, by conforming to His will, participate in that continual act of love. God's knowledge of Himself is love. We have to begin with the faith that we have within ourselves this possibility; and that everything we truly know is (since only reality can be truly known) an aspect of this principial *gnosis*, a light here and there, to increase and deepen the light we already possess. St. Paul declares, "We know in part" until "when that which is perfect is come that which is in part shall be done away." This partial knowledge is the very definition of our world of space and time; for space and time are in existence only for so long as we are not altogether conformed to God's knowing of Himself. Whoever becomes thus conformed has turned earth into heaven and is released from what we call "this world."

Meanwhile, each one of us has within his reach that degree of direct knowledge that he needs and has the capacity to assimilate, no more and no less. He does not need what he cannot or will not use, desperately as he may need to increase his own willingness to use more of so priceless a gift. His receptive capacity is the measure of his conformity to God's will in act and word and thought. It will increase or decrease in accordance with his faithfulness or his indifference. We may be tempted to equate true *gnosis* with a rarefied spirituality and exalted intellectual discourse, rather than with humility and a holy life, but this would be a great mistake. Insofar as a man's life falls short of holiness, his apparent "knowledge" is of no account. Conversely, insofar as the most seemingly inarticulate and foolish individual conforms his thoughts and actions to the will of God, he knows God, albeit in a simple mode. It is God who sends the light which shows the way to Him; and He sends it to the pure in heart, to them always, and to no one else.

There is "knowing" and there is "knowing about." "Knowing about" is the definition of a verbalized kind of knowledge that comes as a result of listening or reading or (less reliably) "insight." A valid tradition both mediates direct knowledge through its images and sacraments and teaches us "about" the relationships in the metaphysical realm and our own situation in relation to that realm. Ideally, this "teaching about" should radiate outwards and downwards from a central religious authority, to include within its scope every discipline, school, and workshop within a given collectivity, with the various collectivities respecting one another's integrity and visualizing the final drawing together of them all in preparation for the metamorphosis of our world into the heavenly state. There is no legitimate division between theology and the skills involved in agriculture or thatching a roof, or between astrophysics and the principles enunciated in the New Testament. Historically, every one of the great traditions has attempted to realize this integration of the various aspects of human life. The results have been fraught with disasters on account of man's sin; even so, they have constituted the nobility of history, little as we are prepared nowadays to admit this as having been the case.

What, then, can we "know about" God?

The first answer must be that the mere notion of knowing anything about God as He is in Himself has a tinge of blasphemy. The second, which is the other side of the paradox, is that whatever we learn about anything is knowledge about God in the sense that God contains the reality of that thing. Tradition teaches us about God in His dealings with our world, so that we may be guided back along the path that leads to Him. This involves certain statements (couched in symbolical terms) relating to those movements within the Godhead without some dim knowledge of which we could not speak of how we came to be. But we must never lose sight of the warning, conveyed to us in many a fairy tale and minor myth, that mere curiosity about holy things is the worst and most dangerous form of self-indulgence.

The Buddha refused to make a single positive statement about God. This refusal is one of the more striking features of Buddhism, for which reason it has often been described by Christians as an "atheistic" religion. Its own scriptures refute this accusation.

There is, disciples, an Unbecome, Unborn, Unmade,
Unformed; if there were not an Unbecome, Unborn,
Unmade, Unformed, there would be no way out for
that which is become, born, made, and formed; but since
there is an Unbecome, Unborn, Unmade, Unformed;
there is escape for that which is become, born, made,
and formed.

Udana viii.1.4,3

In fact, Buddhism is not, in this matter, so far removed
from Christianity as is commonly supposed. "We cannot
know what God is," declared St. Thomas Aquinas, whose
works were for centuries the foundation of Roman Catholic
theology, "but rather what He is not." And the Dominican
Meister Eckhart (1260-1327) wrote: "Aught that a man
could or would think of God, God is not at all." Not, it
should be noted, that we may not aspire to know God
with His own knowledge in the mystical vision, but that
we cannot think *about* Him or know *what* He is. The
Jewish *Kabbalah*, which contains the mystical teachings of
Israel, speaks of the AYIN SOF and the AYIN. AYIN in
Hebrew means "No-thing." God is AYIN. But He is also
AYIN SOF, meaning "the One-without-end." AYIN is prior
to AYIN SOF; so the first, and in a sense the only statement
we are permitted to make "about" God is a total negation;
only after that may we go on to see Him in terms of his
creation, as the All, the One from whom the many have
emerged and to whom the many will return. God is AYIN
SOF. But AYIN SOF is not God.

Meister Eckhart took risks that, in his day, endangered
a man's life. He was under grave suspicion of heresy, not
because he ever spoke an heretical word, but because he
carried certain truths to their extremes in a manner that
was too much for mediocre minds, as, for instance, when
he declared, "God is neither good nor true." The ninth-
century theologian John Scotus Erigena was content to say

the same thing less provocatively: "God does not know what He is, because He is not any what." We should note, however, that neither of these masters at any time said of God that He did not, by direct knowledge, know Himself.

There is, in every known tradition, a prohibition against the casual utterance of whatever word has been set apart as representing the Name of God. (There is, in fact, no such word in English. The word *God*, although it should never be used lightly, is a code word rather than the keystone of a sacred language; and so it does not have the awesome significance of, for instance, the word *Allah*, which one almost hesitates to write.) The reason is that God's Hidden Name, by which He addresses Himself and which is known only to Him, is his primary manifestation. God's Name is God's Word. "Hallowed be thy name"; those words, repeated daily by Christians, echo a theme that recurs constantly in scriptures, prayer, and mystical writings all over the world. Traditionally, the name represents the exteriorization of the interiority of the named: hence the significance in myth and fairytale of knowing a person's name. Nowadays we play havoc with each other's names. But this is a sign of the times: it is more normal to regard the use of the personal name as a privilege because it refers to the person behind the social function represented by his formal designation. How much more, then, should we hesitate to invoke the Name of God. Beyond that Name there is only the pure negativity of the AYIN; therefore, that Name, or rather the word that is used for that Name, is always the central and most numinous of all the words in the sacred language that it is one of the primary tasks of a tradition to initiate. It alone is able to bestow meaning upon all other words by providing the nucleus around which they assemble and order themselves for the purpose of communicating truth. All the words in the language are held to be contained within God's Name or Word, from which they have emerged and to which, in perfect order, rightly related one to the other, they must eventually be drawn back. In the Jewish tradition, none save the High Priest of the Temple, and that but once a year as he stood alone in the innermost sanctuary before the Ark of the Covenant, was permitted to utter the One coordinating Word. For it was said that by the power of that Word the worlds were made, and by its power they will be unmade on the Last Day when all shall be judged.

The scripture known as *Zohar*, which is part of *Kabbalah*, explains, "Because man is not able to picture God as He really is, he is not allowed to represent Him, either by a picture, or by his name, or even by a dot." Here is another universal prohibition. No tradition has ever permitted the pictorial representation of God as He is in Himself. Scandalized reactions on the part of Jews and Muslims faced with Christian paintings of God the Father, either in conjunction with the other Persons of the Trinity or in the act of creation or simply looking down from heaven, are the result of a misunderstanding. Such pictorial images are not intended to be of God "as He really is." They depict the principle of Fatherhood within the Godhead; just as the figure of Siva dancing depicts the eternal interweaving of the opposites within the One. Every religious system has its divine figures representing aspects of God but not God in his ultimate transcendence. If there were no such visualizations, prayer and praise below the level of pure contemplation would be impossible. A beautiful hymn by Gregorius the Theologian expresses the dilemma of the mystic:

> O thou beyond all things
> > what else can it be meet to call thee?
> How can speech praise thee?
> > for thou art not expressible by any speech.

How can reason gather thee?
　　for thou art not comprehensible by any mind.
Thou that art alone ineffable
　　while thou engenderest all that is open to speech.
Thou that alone art unknowable
　　while thou engenderest all that is open to thought...
End of all things art thou
　　and one and all and none,
Not being one nor all, claiming all names
　　how shall I call thee?

4

Which Came First?

"If God exists, why do I?" asked the poet George Barker, voicing what is perhaps the most fundamental of all questions. If, as tradition declares with one voice, in the words of St. John of the Cross, "God permits not that any other thing should dwell together with Him," how is it that I seem to myself to have a separate existence? To answer this question in terms of human logic is impossible. To arrive at a true understanding of it in such a way that the answer is realized in the heart and communicates itself to the mind, one must be willing constantly and persistently to direct the attention to a level transcending that upon which the laws of logic legitimately operate.

Meanwhile, there is available to us, within the various traditions, a vast body of metaphysical speculation on the subject of the mystery of the creation of the world—which can equally well be described as the mystery of why I exist. It is inadvisable to boggle the mind with too much reading on this subject; we should read for the purpose of dispelling, not producing, puzzlement. The principle to be followed is that metaphysical studies are for the practical purpose of leading us in the direction of truth, and should never be pursued further than is appropriate to the present stage of our mental and spiritual development. Always the student should preserve as his main objective the ideal of being simple before God. The great metaphysicians such as Plato and Plotinus, the sages of the Hindu *Vedanta,* and the Jewish authors of *Kabbalah,* who wrote of the ineffable movements within the Godhead that brought the worlds into existence, did so on the understanding that their words would be read solely by those who were able to profit by them. Such works were most unlikely to fall into the hands of the unprepared, passed down as they were from master to disciple within the context of a school. The idea of their being made generally available, together with a miscellaneous assortment of other teachings, as they are today, would have been inconceivable to their authors. In our own times, in the absence of an ordered context within which such studies can be properly directed, it is necessary that wider opportunities should be made available to us; but we need to understand how to use them. The first necessity is to realize the inevitable abnormality of our methods of study, so that we do not abuse the privilege of having so vast a treasure trove of wisdom laid open to us all at once.

Turning our attention, then, to the mystery of our own existence, the first task confronting us will be that of making a correct distinction between the secular sciences of our own time and the multi-dimensional cosmologies that grew up within the context of the ancient wisdom. A great deal of unnecessary bewilderment has been produced both by those who would suggest that scientific discoveries have not only "disproved" the traditional cosmologies but have undermined religious belief to the extent of making it redundant—and, more recently, by a fashion for juxtaposing

our own world view (as the norm) with selected passages
from the ancient scriptures of East and West in a manner
designed, somewhat patronizingly, to demonstrate that our
forefathers saw through a glass darkly what we see face
to face. Nothing could be further from the truth. Our
forefathers perceived the cosmos as a holy book containing
the primordial revelation of a multi-level reality, the higher
reaches of which are unseen and can be studied only by
means of a unified science unfolding from a metaphysical
point of view. Starting from this point of view, they
developed symbolic pictures of the cosmic reality which
owed their validity to the fact that primordial nature—
from the starry heavens to the molecular structure of a
cell—is a unified system of correspondences, a theophany
which is capable not only of communicating blessedness
to the simple, but of revealing universal laws to the
practitioners of the various disciplines that are, or should
be, part of the "one kind of knowledge"—the knowledge
of the ways of God.

Those disciplines, which would formerly have included
research into the mysteries concealed in such intangibles
as number, rhythm, measurement, and sound, and the
spiritual and psychical effects of different materials and
shapes, are needed for the practical purpose of our survival
upon earth. They are needed as contributions to the sum
of human wisdom, provided always that they remain in
the hands of the wise, who will pass them on in accordance
with the capacities of those who are fit and willing to be
taught. The work of observation and experimentation on
the physical level, which is the legitimate aspect of
contemporary science, should not be allowed to issue in
the kind of philosophizing that has no anchor in traditional
metaphysics. Modern man has made an idol of this science
of the material world because it serves his own Promethean
view of himself, paradoxically, by emphasizing his

quantitative insignificance in the universe. This notion destroys not only his true dignity but the idea of his one unassailable "rival," the God in whose image he was made. At the same time it enables him to aspire to "conquer" the infinities of the cosmos and the mysteries of life and death. So small and yet potentially so omnipotent is how man sees himself in relation to the stars. A more balanced view of reality would integrate the physical sciences within a metaphysical framework, while restricting scientific research in accordance with the grades imposed by a school that would rate spiritual qualifications as vital to the achievement of its degrees. Nowadays we are witnessing the extraordinary spectacle of a science that seems as if it were battering on the doors of the metaphysical and finding them closed. Limiting ourselves to the material, we have come to the limits of the material. We have started from the bottom, and found ourselves at that place where our chosen method reveals itself as being inadequate. A science of relentless experimentation to discover the nature of material objects has been forced to conclude that there is no such thing as a material object. The observed world is, they tell us, an artifact of the subject-object relationship. Our forefathers knew this quite well; what they also knew was that, beyond the possibility of experiment or of "proof," there exists a reality of which the observed world is both a veil and a manifestation, and a knowledge that is based upon faith.

Metaphysical truths are expressible only in terms of symbolism and myth. Hence the traditional sciences were contained within the framework of a cosmic symbolism that differed from one to another of the great religions while, in each case, pointing to primordial truths transcending the literal interpretation of the imagery in question. Within such a system the physical sciences would function as the servants, not the arbiters, of truth. It is (as our astro-

physicists are beginning to find out) no more absolutely
true to say that the earth goes round the sun than it is to
change the symbolism by putting the matter the other way
round. Both of these ideas are based upon appearances
conditioned by our limited sensory apparatus, the former
being more "useful" in the practical sense because it is based
upon more data and can be related to a far more
comprehensive system of illusion (creation being at the same
time reality *and* illusion: reality as the manifestation of
God's attributes; illusion insofar as we treat our own limited
apprehensions of it as being absolute). The notion that there
is any possibility of the physical sciences "disproving"
anything that is integral to a valid symbolic system arises
on the one hand from a too literal and historical approach
to such systems, on the other from ascribing an absolute
value to what is merely an appearance, albeit one of infinite
significance, if we but understood it for what it is. (The
latter mistake is still prevalent among scientists attached to
the minor disciplines, despite its incompatibility with
quantum physics. The fact is that science itself is in a vast
confusion, torn between two conflicting points of view,
neither of which has any room for the Divine Reality that
transcends them both.)

We have already mentioned the priority in terms of
reality of the greater over the lesser; the function of praise
and the manifestation of freedom in flight as being more
fundamental to the behavior of a bird than the practical
necessities which are the physical "causes" of this behavior
from the point of view of ornithological research. The
greatest danger in the contemporary scientific approach to
the mysteries of the natural world is that it leads us to regard
the phenomena of causation from below upwards, as if it
were possible that a tree could be the product of a seed
or the universe of a "big bang" without the reality of the
universe and of the tree having pre-existed the physical

"causes" of these phenomena in the world of space and time. Thus we acquire a false notion of the meaning of nature and of ourselves, or rather, we lose the idea of there being a meaning in nature and in ourselves. For what is apparent to us in nature is but a partial and misleading truth until we are prepared to see nature in the light of our knowledge of God. Meister Eckhart expressed the matter succinctly when he wrote, "Nature forms the man from the child and the hen from the egg, but God makes the man before the child and the hen before the egg."

And Rumi, in one of the most beautiful of his poems, expressed the same thought:

> Externally the branch is the origin of the fruit;
> intrinsically the branch came into existence
> for the sake of the fruit.
> Had there been no hope of the fruit
> would the gardener have planted the tree?
> Therefore in reality the tree is born of the fruit
> though it appear to be produced by the tree.

Here the external and the interior or intrinsic meanings of the natural objects in question are contrasted in such a way that we are enabled to see the priority in terms of origin and in terms of nobility of the latter over the former. It is, therefore, more important to understand the latter than to analyze the former. A child should be able to look at a natural object and perceive, as Rumi did, its interior meaning as a manifestation of the Divine, growing out of and returning to the completion (the fruiting tree) from which it came forth, long before there is any question of pulling that object to pieces to see how it "works." Children naturally observe nature in this way. They participate in its meaning, and will continue to do so for so long as their minds are not distorted by the itch to interfere with it and

pull it about. Under the tyranny imposed by the modern
idolization of the "scientific" viewpoint (which is in reality
the viewpoint of what should be the most menial and
humble of all the scientific methods in existence), this
distortion takes place very early. A small child who watches
a moon landing on television or assists in the laboratory
dissection of a frog will be, unless he has carried with him
into incarnation an exceptional strength to resist the
pressures exerted upon him, unable ever again to look at
the moon or at frogs or at anything else in the world of
nature with the pure, untarnished vision that sees things
as they really are. It is the outward form of a natural object
as seen by us in the context of our natural environment
that unfolds into manifestation the interior meaning of that
object, the reality to which it corresponds. Thus the moon
in the sky is more beautiful and more meaningful (which
is the same thing) than the moon "discovered" by methods
which are unnatural and illegitimate because they are being
undertaken without proper spiritual preparation and outside
the restraining context of an all-embracing science based
upon metaphysical truth. Similarly a frog leaping and
croaking in the garden is a thing of wonder touched by
a ray of the Divine; splayed out on the laboratory table
it is a sight unfit for anyone but a student of the higher
wisdom, whose spiritual qualifications have bestowed upon
him the right to undertake this type of research.

We are speaking now of an ideal so far removed from
our present-day situation as to seem almost impossible of
fulfillment. Nevertheless we should realize that it is the ideal
that is simple and normal, and our own taken-for-granted
way of conducting ourselves that is outrageous. We may
conclude these considerations with a quotation from the
chapter entitled "The Cosmos as Theophany" in *Knowledge
and the Sacred* [1] by Seyyed Hossein Nasr, the leading
scholarly interpreter of Sufism at the present time: "One

wonders who knows more about the coyote, the zoologist who is able to study its external habits and dissect its cadaver or the Indian medicine man who identifies himself with the 'spirit' of the coyote?"

5

What Really Happened?

There can be no scientific description of creation because creation is, by definition, a metaphysical event. The "big bang" (if it took place) was not the creation of the worlds, any more than the coming together of sperm and ovum is the creation of the human being who will be formed as a result. "God makes the man before the child," and He made all things in their perfection before the "big bang." The act of creation has been described in every one of the great traditions; indeed, it seems improbable that there has ever existed a religious system, however primitive, which lacks such a description. But no one has ever been able to describe what "happened" except in mythological terms. When *Kabbalah* declares that God withdrew Himself from Himself in order to make a void which became the mirror of Himself, or when Plato, in *Timaeus*, produces an account of the making of the worlds and of the human soul in terms of mathematical computations, these explanations, compared with the countless stories of gods and goddesses that modern man dismiss as mere childish tales, are but a more intellectualized and sophisticated type of myth. We cannot describe or explain metaphysical reality except in terms of our own experience. Realizing this limitation in ourselves liberates us on the one hand from the tendency to interpret a symbolic description literally and historically; on the other from the temptation to dismiss such descriptions, when we can no longer interpret them literally and historically, as being "untrue."

Given this situation, it is legitimate to ask whether there is enough in common between the principal mythological accounts of the first moment of creation for us to derive from them some image that we can understand and appreciate, as a reassurance that they are all, in their different ways, bearing witness to the same event. If we look in turn at *Kabbalah*, Plato, the Hindu *Vedanta*, the sayings of Muhammad, the book of Genesis, and the gospel of St. John, we shall find in all these writings the same basic idea of a movement within the Godhead whereby God contemplates Himself. God, as it were, goes out from and returns to Himself in an act of love. Hinduism conceives of this movement as the outgoing and indrawing of a breath. The outgoing breath is the utterance of the word OM, which is the sum of all being. Dispersed in time and space, the OM produces all the things that are; drawn back whence it came, it carries with it all that it became in time. Genesis, which seems to begin at a point "after" the Kabbalistic void has been brought into existence (if, indeed, a void can be said to "exist"; the word is clearly inaccurate, and its very inaccuracy is significant), speaks first of a light that moves upon the face of darkness, reflecting God's image back to itself. This image takes the form of androgynous man. Man is poised in a momentary perfection within the context of a perfect world, before succumbing to the principle of duality that is within him, because it is in God, and that his God-given freedom enables him to exploit, take

advantage of, and misuse. St. John the Evangelist makes
use of a similar concept to that of the OM, the Greek *Logos*
("Word"), familiar to his contemporaries as defining the
creative outgoingness of God. "In the beginning was the
Word, and the Word was with God and the Word was
God... And the Word was made flesh."

Christian mythology emphasizes the mysterious
paradox that creation is a movement whereby God
withdraws from and returns to Himself within the Godhead
which He has never left. The Word is made flesh; but the
Word is both the incarnate Christ, and the second person
of the Trinity, who remains in the heart of the Godhead
with the Father and the Holy Spirit. The Christian Trinity
is an image of love. Its movement within itself brings about
creation. The flesh-taking of the Word is represented,
ambiguously, as being the very fact of the creation of the
Perfect Man, and as a necessity brought about by the Fall
into sin. So we pass almost immediately from the first
Mystery to the idea of a restoration of unity following the
appearance of a flaw in the order of God's world. This will
prove to be one of the most difficult of all metaphysical
ideas for the mind to assimilate, because it can be expressed
only by means of a mythology that defies all our precon-
ceived notions of time, logic, and the laws of cause and
effect. As we penetrate that mythology, step-by-step, it is
necessary to hold fast to the idea of the simultaneity of
everything that transcends the dimensions of our space and
time. Creation, incarnation, restoration, are a single act from
the point of view of God. Our problem is that we cannot,
in this life, achieve that absolutely central, absolutely
transcendent point of view.

At the heart of the Christian mythology of creation
is the image of the Blessed Virgin Mary, upon whom—
and upon her sinful counterpart, the wandering Magdalen,
who typifies the *process* or creation in time as distinct from

the creative act—our attention must be turned as we consider this subject in the light of the Church's teaching. In fact there has been associated with the idea of creation in virtually every known tradition a divine or semi-divine female figure, the Holy Femininity, who appears in various guises as mother, daughter, virgin, bride, but always as a partner in the sacred acts. In the Christian revelation, She is ultimately indistinguishable from the third person of the Trinity, the *Sancta Sophia*, the Holy Spirit. We cannot, of course, aspire to penetrate more than a very little way into secrets so ineffable as this. But without a glimpse of their meaning, we shall understand nothing of what the Church has to say about our origin and end. No matter what aspect of reality we are studying at any given moment, we are bound to include in our studies the Mystery of the Femininity of God.

The Feminine Mystery has a dual aspect. Hinduism has its Parvati, the Beautiful, whose counterpart is Kali, the Dark Goddess, both of them brides of the same God, who is Himself Creator and Destroyer of the worlds. Again and again, across the traditions, the same pattern is repeated with innumerable variations. In esoteric Christianity the two Maries are reunited at the end of time, in the Assumption of the Virgin and her Coronation as the Bride of Christ. Mary Magdalene (whose Assumption is an arcane teaching seldom made explicit) is identical with the Jewish Shekinah, who wanders in exile, invaded by seven devils and grieving for her lost love. Mary the Virgin, flawless "mirror" of the divine effulgence, is the timeless Sophia (Wisdom) of the Old Testament, who assists in the work of creation, being Herself the pre-existent pattern for that work. The Roman Catholic Missal makes this identification by its choice of the lessons for the Feast of the Immaculate Conception and that of the Assumption, both being taken from the Wisdom literature of the Old Testament. The doctrine of the Immaculate Conception implies that the Virgin was conceived in a dimension including, yet transcending, that of time—in the first moment of creation and, simultaneously, in the womb of her mother St. Anne. The meaning is that she is the one perfectly sinless creature, inheriting no tendency to sin because her generation precedes the appearance of sin. (It is also said that, as the daughter of human parents, she was redeemed, in the moment of her conception by the retrospective action of her Son: this is to look at the Mystery from another point of view, which will not confuse us if we understand the simultaneity of all the 'events' that appear to follow one another in the sacred myth.) In the lesson for this feast, taken from the Book of Proverbs, she declares:

> The Lord possessed me in the beginning of his ways, before He made anything, from the beginning. I was set up from eternity, and of old, before the earth was made. The depths were not as yet, and I was already conceived; neither had the fountains of waters as yet sprung out; the mountains with their huge bulk had not as yet been established: before the hills I was brought forth; He had not yet made the earth, nor the rivers, nor the poles of the world. When He prepared the heavens I was there; when with a certain law and compass He enclosed the depths; when He established the sky above, and poised the fountains of waters; when He compassed the sea with its bounds, and set a law to the waters that they should not pass their limits; when He balanced the foundations of the earth, I was with Him, forming all things, and was delighted every day, playing before Him at all times, playing in the world: and my delight is to be with the children of men...'

This semi-divine Sophia derives her being from the Holy Spirit, whose vessel she is: the Spirit Itself is the Sancta

Sophia who gives her its own Name. In the Book of Wisdom it is written of her that she 'passeth and goeth through all things by reason of her pureness... therefore can no defiled thing fall into her': a double statement which turns round upon itself, meaning that perfect purity is perfect passability; it cannot be tarnished by anything with which it comes into contact. Nowadays we have trivialised the idea of purity, as we have materialised that of virginity, with the result that the figure of Mary has been completely misunderstood. Purity is translucency. It is the capacity of water to hold a clear reflection, of a glass vessel to contain water in such a way that the glass appears to be the water, and both are invisible save in terms of what is reflected within them. Purity is absolute nonresistance. Mary represents our humanity as it was, and is, and will be, in God, untampered with by sin. "In her we see our pure nature," wrote St. Louis de Monfort (1673-1716), whose exceptional devotion to Our Lady resulted in his canonization by Pius XII. Her part in creation is to represent its state of perfection, being in Herself the pre-existent reality of that perfection, "before" the Fall into sin. We cannot do without this archetype of blessedness, to recall us again and again to a realization of our exiled state.

Mary Magdalene, the "other face" of Mary, is the type of that exile, and of the pilgrimage of the soul in search of the lost Beloved. Without her the Virgin-in-time is incomplete. In the moment of creation she is freed to go her lonely way until creation's consummation at the end of time. Then, and then only, will the two Maries once again be one. This idea is worked out in various ways, with almost incredible ramifications within the Gnostic schools that were contemporaneous with the early Church. The association of these schools with mainstream Christianity is a subject which may never now be unravelled. (The destruction of the great library at Alexandria in the fifth century A.D. probably removed the key to this, as to so much else.) Condemned as heretical by the Fathers of the Church, they cast a light upon the gospel story which reveals the latter as cloaking arcane Mysteries beneath what appear to be historical episodes and relationships — such as, for instance, the friendship between Jesus and the Magdalen.

The Samaritan Simon Magus, a contemporary of the apostles and regarded by the early Fathers as an arch-heretic, wrote of the fallen Ennoia (who is both the exiled Shekinah and the fallen Sophia):

> [She] was dragged down from the highest heavens into the cosmos. And she suffered all manner of abuse . . . that she might not return upward to her Father . . . and migrated for centuries as from vessel to vessel into different female bodies . . . Migrating from body to body, suffering abuse in each, she at last became a whore in a brothel, and this is the "lost sheep."

It is also, unmistakably, Mary the Prostitute. Catholic popular tradition enshrines many so-called "heresies" in such a way that those who have eyes to see can perceive them as being, in reality, part of the very basis of the myth. We do not have to immerse ourselves in the bewildering complexities of Gnosticism (indeed, it would be most inadvisable for most of us to do anything of the kind) in order to recognize that the two Maries are one Mary as seen under two aspects and from two differing points of view — as the soul serene in God, and as the soul on her way back to that original, and final, state, which in a sense she has never left. Countless representations of the Assumption of the Virgin in Christian art are paralleled by a few rare paintings of the Assumption of the Magdalen, naked and covered by her flowing hair. One such picture is sufficient to convince us. For what other saint was ever accorded the honor due to Mary of being assumed bodily into heaven?

This reunion of the two Maries in heaven is the return of creation to its source. There was no-thing in between: only time, which is an illusion born of our folly in believing that the no-thing which is ourselves is a some-thing that is other than God to be set up as a rival to Him. That is the illusion that keeps the second Mary wandering as an exile in time, prostituting the love that is for the "one thing only" upon a multitude of objects that will prove to have been worthless. For what purpose was she created, save to return the love of the one true subject-object of love – the Eternal Word, who, in Christian terminology, is called the Christ? The Word is the expression of Divine Love, the pure creative act that brings into manifestation that aspect of the Godhead that, of its essential nature, wills to manifest itself.

> OM,
> The imperishable sound,
>   is the seed of all that exists.
> The past, the present, the future,
>   – all are but the unfolding of OM.
> And whatever transcends the three worlds of time,
>   that indeed is the flowering of OM...
> *Mandukya Upanishad*

There are so many marvelous passages in the scriptures of the world and in the writings of the mystics which speak of this Mystery of the creating Word that one hardly knows how to choose from among them.

> Utterance brought forth all the universe.
> He pronounced *Bhu* ("Earth") and the earth was born.
> *Satapatha-Brahmana*

The seventh-century Hindu philosopher and poet Bhartrhari observes, "All this Universe is but the result of sound" (Vakya Padiya 1.24), a truth which is nowadays being rediscovered on the plane of physics, with the reduction of apparent substantiality to a mind-blowing pattern of vibrations. The Oath of Initiation, which is one of the very few texts that remain to us from the Mysteries of Eleusis, was: "So help me heaven, the work of God who is both great and wise: so help me the word of the Father which he spake when he established the universe in his wisdom."

St. Francis de Sales, Bishop of Geneva in the early part of the seventeenth century, was not going contrary to the findings of modern science, but rather seeing matters from a timeless point of view, when he wrote:

> God spoke but one word, and in virtue of that in a moment were made the sun, moon, and that innumerable multitude of stars, with their differences in brightness, motion, and influence. *He spoke and they were made* (Psalm CXLVIII.5). A single word of God's filled the air with birds, and the sea with fishes, made spring from the earth all the plants and all the beasts we see . . .

What a fearful loss have we sustained, that we can no longer see this vision as presenting a reality far greater and more substantial than the pictures conjured up by a science of merely physical "cause and effect." Let us turn once more to Meister Eckhart: "The heavenly Father speaks but one Word and that he speaks eternally and in this Word expends he all his might: his entire God-nature he utters in this Word, and the whole of creatures."

6

How Then Came Sin?

How then came sin? How came the disorder and
suffering that broke into the fair beauty of God's first
creation on account of sin?

Once again, finding ourselves in the realm of the
metaphysical, we must seek for "explanations" in terms of
symbolism and myth. For Christians the story begins in
the book of Genesis. The serpent tells Adam and Eve that
if they eat the fruit of the Tree of the Knowledge of Good
and Evil, they will be "as gods." Thus the idea of duality
leads to opposition. Androgynous man was divided into
two, in his sleep, "before" the temptation by the serpent.
This division of the previously united man-woman leads
(although it need not have done so) to a further step, that
of desiring to know the opposites in a state of conflict and
to manipulate the powers released in that conflict. Man
("the Adam")[1] sets himself up as the rival of his creator
insofar as he aspires to wield the forces of creation and
destruction by his own hands. (How can man sustain the
balance? He cannot.) Another and parallel myth, that of

the Archangel Lucifer, explains the origin of evil in terms
of the pride of the greatest of all the angels, the Prince of
Light, who counted himself equal with God, and so was
flung downwards into the nethermost abyss.

Duality is nowhere represented as being in itself an evil
state. In itself it is a transitory aspect of the process initiated
by the creative act. Even "before" that act took place, the
One was divided in two, thus producing a third and
becoming the Trinity of Love. (This truth is the essential
metaphysical basis of the Church's prohibition against
contraception; when the origin of the prohibition is
understood there will be, for the first time, some prospect
of modifying it without sacrificing the meaning concealed
within its symbolism.) In *Kabbalah*, the central image is
that of the Sephirotic Tree, on opposite branches of which
the divine attributes descend in pairs, in perfect equilibrium,
from the One. The dance of Siva, which is the principal
visual image of Hinduism, depicted again and again in the
highly formalized statuary of the temple, symbolizes the
energies of creation and destruction perpetually weaving
and working together to bring about that state of balance
between the two which is the condition of existence. It
is the upsetting of that balance, as a consequence of human
sin, that brings about what we call "evil," which is in itself
a no-thing, a void where (impossibly, but so we must
express it) God is not. Justice and mercy, for instance, typify
a duality that issues in conflict only when the one
overbalances the other, resulting in the opposition of an
"evil" to a weakened, ineffectual "good." In the Christian
Mystery, the balance destroyed by man is instantaneously
restored by God who, as Redeeming Christ, holds it
together on the Cross.

The idea of the Fall is inseparable from that of free
will and the abuse of free will. Man, the apex of creation,
has had bestowed upon him the power to choose. No other

creature has been granted that privilege. Man must choose between two alternatives; there is no third. Shall he be the no-thing-in-God that is destined to be deified in God (as Mary, in her Assumption into heaven, becomes the Bride of Christ) or shall he attempt to be himself-by-himself? The sin of Lucifer is the sin of man's spiritual being, that highest part of his nature that raises him to the level of the angels, at the same time deluding him into the belief that he is self-sufficient. (A second version of the Luciferian Fall describes how the great archangel refused to bow down to the newly created form of man when commanded to do so by God. The meaning here is that man's intellectual power refuses to be the servant of God's image in his heart as manifested in his outward form, but demands to be supreme and independent.) It is in his higher nature that man sins, not as a corporate body, as "mankind," but as one individual human soul alone with God, at that point where the soul of each one of us coincides with the "Adam" who is the prototype of us all.

This point of co-incidence is the intersection of eternity with time. It is the point of the Cross, the point of all the "Mysteries" of the Christian faith, the point of what the Church defines as "original sin" or the "origin" of sin. The sins that we daily commit are the result of our primary sin; they represent its power over us, being in themselves the occasions when we submit ourselves temporarily to that power. In Roman Catholic moral theology a distinction used to be drawn between "mortal" and "venial" sin. The meaning of this distinction is that it is theoretically possible for the individual totally and deliberately to re-identify himself with his own "original" sin, in denial of the saving grace of the Spirit in Christ, and in such a way as to have no intention of returning to that grace. This is the state of "mortal" sin; and those theologians who still understand their own teachings will freely admit that for most of us,

living as we do in a state of weakness and ineffectuality,
this theoretical possibility, if it is ever in fact actualized,
is a mercifully rare phenomenon. We dare not, however,
on that account, assume ourselves to be incapable of it.
Nowadays one does not hear the expression "mortal sin."
Like almost every other teaching that refers to a
metaphysical idea, it has been discounted because its
meaning has become obscured by the literal and legalistic
interpretations forced upon it.

It may be useful at this point to explain the
metaphysical basis of the sacrament of Penance, which has
given rise to fundamental misunderstandings both inside
and outside the Roman Catholic Church. In the days before
Vatican II the teaching was clear enough, if painfully
literalistic. Confession was obligatory solely in the case of
"mortal" sin. It constituted the sacrament whereby the state
of soul brought about by a fully deliberate and God-defying
sin could be undone by means of repentance, confession,
and the absolution of the Holy Spirit. But how was one
supposed to distinguish for oneself between "mortal" sins,
which must be confessed, and "venial" sins, which were in
an altogether different category of seriousness? The Church
solved this problem by producing a literal and terrifying
definition of "mortal" sin as any deliberate act or omission
involving disobedience to the laws of God as interpreted
by the ecclesiastical authority—from committing murder
to missing Sunday Mass. The extraordinary state of mind
that would actually be involved in the real commission of
a "mortal" sin tended, under this alarming dispensation, to
be overlooked. A further source of misunderstanding was
the automatic categorization of all unorthodox sexual
relationships as "living in sin." This categorization had far
more to do with the idea of protracted disobedience than
with a disproportionate condemnation of extramarital sex;
but the matter was seldom explained in those terms; and

the misunderstanding was not restricted to those outside the Church. The penalty for unrepented "mortal" sin was stated to be cosignment to hell. Given a true understanding of the meaning of this statement, it may well be true. In the context of so literal and legalistic an interpretation of the nature of this category of sin, the idea is not only merciless but preposterous.[2] Probably the majority of Catholics recognized it as being so, and went to Confession from motives quite other than that of preserving themselves from everlasting punishment. The most beautiful and profoundly mystical aspect of this sacrament consists in the idea that one's actual sins can become the sacramental "matter" to be transformed into the transfigured Body of the Son of God. The whole of the material and psychical world, on every level of its existence, is destined to be redeemed in Christ; and in this transfiguration every action, every thought, insofar as one turns it back to God, to be transformed by Him in the sacrifice which is symbolized for Christians by the Mass, will have its proper place. This is the inner meaning of the routine confession of a "washing list" of "venial" sins. Now that meaning, together with the metaphysical idea at the basis of the Church's wildly distorted teachings on "mortal" sin, has virtually been lost. Confession is reduced to a sentimental exercise in counseling and reassurance, all the more foolish in that a priest, as such, has no particular skills as an amateur psychologist.

The *Revelations* of Julian of Norwich, more lucidly perhaps than any other work of Christian mysticism, depict, in the form of a simple story simply told, the simultaneity of the diverse aspects of the primal act of love. Julian describes her perplexity on account of the existence of sin within a total reality which she comprehended as being good ("for our soul is so fully oned to God of His own goodness that between God and our soul may be right nought") and how she prayed for a revelation to ease her mind and was granted "none other answer but a marvellous example of a lord and of a servant. . .and that full mistily shewed."

Julian was one of the great metaphysicians of all time. She has been grievously misrepresented by sentimentalists, who have emphasized her tenderness without her acerbity, but above all have failed to grasp the outstanding intellectual clarity and subtlety of her exposition of the blinding paradoxes at the heart of Truth. With unwavering sureness she finds her way between the seeming contradictions, reconciling them with childlike simplicity, but in each case with an answer that no learned philosopher would be qualified to dispute. One is left with the conviction that she, " a simple creature unlettered," did indeed receive a revelation directly from God. Of all her "shewings," the one of "a Lord that hath a servant" is perhaps the most astonishing in its combination of intellectual subtlety with naivety of expression; it is also completely "original," not in the sense of being a curiosity outside the mainstream of the Christian tradition, but in being a pure expression of the truth of the heart. The chapters in which it is recounted and explained must be read in their entirety (preferably in one of the older editions which adhere as closely as is practicable to the language of the original) if their full meaning is to be absorbed. Here we can do no more than summarize their contents.

Julian tells us that she saw first (in her spiritual understanding, not as a visual apparition) a simple scene wherein a Lord sent his servant on an errand; and the servant, running in haste, fell into a ravine and was grievously hurt and unable to move. Julian is led to understand that no blame attaches to the servant, but that his Lord pities and loves him all the more on account of his pain. "Yea, and so far forth, that his falling and his woe, that he hath taken thereby, shall be turned into high and overpassing worship and endless bliss." She realizes that the servant "was shewed for Adam" and is immediately convinced that this "example" (as she calls it) contains the solution to the paradox of sin by which she has been grievously perplexed. In the course of the next twenty years she receives "teaching inwardly" to elucidate the many layers of meaning of a scene which at its first level the tiniest child could have understood. The essence of this deeper understanding is that the servant is both the original Adam *and* the Christ.

> In the Servant is comprehended the Second Person of the Trinity; and in the servant is comprehended Adam: that is to say All-man . . . When Adam fell, God's Son fell: because of the rightful oneing which had been made in heaven, God's Son might not be disparted from Adam. Adam fell from life to death into the deep of this wretched world, and after that into hell:[3] God's Son fell with Adam, into the deep of the Maiden's womb . . . to excuse Adam from blame in heaven and in earth; and mightily he fetched him out of hell . . . For in all this our good Lord shewed His own Son and Adam but one Man.

Julian concludes her exposition by declaring, "In this marvellous example I have teaching with me as it were the beginning of an ABC . . . For the secret things of the Revelation be hid therein . . ." In other words, more is implied than even she has, so far, been able to understand; she will have the example with her always, so that she may continue to draw out its inexhaustible meaning for the rest of her life. We may well do the same. All the Mysteries—of simultaneity, of contradiction in unity, of the outgoing of the Word in creation and its return in restoration—that comprise the "secret things" of the Christian revelation are, as she says, contained in the example. It implies, although Julian does not explicitly draw attention to this, that the

Fall of Man and the descent of the creative Word into the
void ("the deep of the Maiden's womb") are two aspects
of the same event.

The Fall into sin is, as it were, the "negative" of
creation's "positive." As such, it is inevitable, as well as being
the outcome of man's freedom of choice. (This is the type
of paradox which the human mind is not constructed to
be able to comprehend, but which can be realized in the
place of the heart and seen clearly as being the truth.) There
is no creation without a fall. The fall of God Himself into
the pure void brings into being man, and the possibility
of man's sin; and since all possibilities must be actualized
in God, sin itself must be actualized in Him. But God
cannot sin in the sense of denying Himself. He receives
sin as suffering and transforms it; and it is in this act that
He is made man, at that point where the human nature
of man reaches up to be united with the Spirit that delivers
him from sin. This is the Mystery of the Passion. It is (as
the Church has always been careful to define) Christ's
manhood that suffers ignominy and pain. His manhood
points the way that man must follow, transforming sin,
through suffering, into "endless bliss." Not that the Godhead
suffers, but that its union with our human nature effects
in us the transformation of suffering. In this way the Christ-
principle is born and brought to maturity in the individual
man, who is himself reborn in it. Thus man, in his
acceptance of suffering, unites the divine and the human
natures in himself. All this and more is contained in that
simple scene of "the Lord that hath a Servant."

A question that has been asked down through the
centuries and has caused bewilderment in many Christians,
relates to the connection between our bodily nature and
the Fall into sin. Was the Fall itself a descent into matter
from the realms of spirit? Even from among the most
orthodox theologians, conflicting answers have been

produced. But through all the controversies, the Church has held to its position of condemning as heretical any version of Christianity which denies, or seems to deny, the final sanctification of the body of man in the Body of Christ."The Word was made flesh." This teaching, and that of the bodily resurrection of the Son of Man, making possible for all men the "resurrection of the body," as affirmed in the creed that has been repeated Sunday after Sunday in churches of all the major denominations, are basic tenets of the Christian faith. On this account, the various breakaway movements generally grouped together as "gnostic," together with the great Catharist "heresy" of the twelfth and thirteenth centuries, all of which were marked by a violent repudiation of the flesh, were fiercely condemned (and in the case of the Albigensian Cathars, mercilessly obliterated) by the Church. Yet it is in what we know of these movements that we find the clearest available evidence for a number of the more esoteric teachings implicit in the gospels, including, for instance, such mysterious pairings as the two Maries, the two Josephs, and the two St. Johns. Hardly can the Church afford to lose such major contributions to its own understanding of itself. The extreme distaste for the physical body that found exppression in gnosticism, leading to a denial that Christ suffered and died upon the Cross (the Christ-principle, it was said, departed from Jesus before it could be subjected to so physical an insult) was, like many another so-called "heresy," an overemphasis upon one side of a paradox that can be held in balance only by a sustained fidelity to the metaphysical point of view. When that point of view is permitted to waver, there is inevitably an imbalance.

What the Gnostics saw only too clearly were the evils inseparable from the descent of the soul into the density and darkness of this world, where it suffers ignominy and insult. Matter, in the Christian tradition, stands for the state of heaviness and impenetrability at the bottom of the scale of being. How, they asked, could it be other than a disaster for the soul to find itself imprisoned in such a state? What they failed to see was that the entry of the Divine Principle into the body in the Incarnation is undertaken for the purpose of restoring the body to the dignity proper to it. The body is not to be equated with "matter" (which will ultimately prove to have been an illusion, a point on which the ancient wisdom and quantum physics are in full agreement); it is rather the Divine Form of the God-man, into which the forms of all men and of all creation will finally be raised up. This body has been dragged down into illusory materiality by man's sin: Christ, the Word, descends with it; and it becomes (as it always was) his own. Ironically, it is its very concern with the body and its importance, which has resulted in the Church's disproportionate preoccupation with bodily sins and with historical facts. All imbalances of emphasis become heresy when carried to extremes. Those Gnostics who spoke of the body as if it were nothing but a container of excrement were as heretical, neither more nor less, as those present-day Christians who advocate continuous "celebration" of the body as if there were no need to pass first through the absolute negation of the Cross.

It was St. Augustine who wrote, "The Word became flesh that flesh might become Word."

That statement is no heresy, but neither is the great poem of the Sufi Ibn Sina (called Avicenna in medieval Europe), describing the descent of the spiritual principle into the human body, which precedes and brings about the creation of the worlds: the light divine that is caught and imprisoned in matter, but has the power to rise again, bearing with it "all hidden things in the universe." This light is sometimes called Word, sometimes Spirit. The distinction between Word and Spirit, the second and third persons

of the Christian Trinity, corresponds to that between the
word spoken and the breath upon which it is spoken. As
a Sufi, Avicenna does not use the trinitarian system. He
declares that the higher soul is a spiritual principle united
with the Divine Spirit but implanted in a material body,
where it remains temporarily imprisoned until it is set free
to return to its heavenly source. This image applies equally
to the implantation of Spirit in a fallen world. "Matter"
is brought into existence by the Fall. If the world of the
first moment of creation is pure void, reflecting back the
light, the world of what we must think of as the "next"
moment imprisons that light. The moment "after" that is
redemption; meanwhile the world as-it-is-in-itself is the
chaos of formless materiality which is, in reality, no reality
but the product of sin and ignorance.

   Avicenna addresses what may be thought of as the
lower soul, describing the descent upon it of the Divine
Principle in union with its own higher self:

> It descended upon thee from out of the regions above,
> That exalted, ineffable, glorious heavenly Dove.
> 'Twas concealed from the eyes of all those who its nature
> would ken
> Yet it wears not a veil, and is ever apparent to men . . .
> It weeps when it thinks of its home and the peace it
> possessed,
> With tears welling forth from its eyes without pausing
> or rest . . .
> Thick nets detain it, and strong is the cage whereby
> It is held from seeking the lofty and spacious sky,
> Until when the hour of its homeward flight draws near,
> And 'tis time for it to return to its ampler sphere,
> It carols with joy, for the veil is raised and it spies
> Such things as cannot be witnessed by waking eyes . . .
> And so it returneth, aware of all hidden things
> In the universe, while no stain to its garment clings . . .

Julian, too, speaks of the higher soul as being released, in the moment of death, into a state of renewed purity and innocence:

> And in this time I saw a body lying on the earth, which body shewed heavy and horrible, without shape and form, as it were a swollen quag of stinking mire. And suddenly out of this body sprang a full fair creature, a little Child, fully shapen and formed, nimble and lively, whiter than lily; which swiftly glided up into heaven. And the swollenness of the body betokeneth great wretchedness of our deadly flesh, and the littleness of the Child betokeneth the cleanness of purity in the soul. And methought: *With this body abideth no fairness of this Child, and on this Child dwelleth no foulness of this body.*

It is not, the mystics seem to be telling us, that we do not have to work out our destiny, making recompense for our sins, in the bonds of time (purgatory, karma, there are many names for that necessity), but that as we rise into eternity, if only for an instant before the cycles of becoming begin to turn for us again, we know ourselves to be as we really are—in God.

What Is Man?

"So God created man in his own image, in the image of God created he him . . ."

There can surely be no more awesome words in the language than these from the King James version of the book of Genesis. They are echoed again and again in the great traditions. "God created Adam in his own form" is one of the sayings of Muhammad. The same teaching is implicit in Hinduism; the art and mythologies of China, Egypt, Persia, and classical Greece proclaimed it. Indeed, it is a truth universally known wherever tradition has perpetuated the ancient wisdom. Man (the original "Adam" before the division into male and female polarized his functions and to that extent modified his perfection) is not merely the apex of creation; he *is* creation. He is God's image, not in the pale reflective sense, as when I see myself in a glass, but because, as Meister Eckhart expresses it, "When God made man, the innermost heart of the Godhead was put into man." This Mystery applies to each and every one of us. The *Zohar* makes this comment upon the statement in Genesis: "It is this image which receives us first, when we come into this world, it develops with us while we grow, and accompanies us when we leave the earth. Its source is in heaven."

The strange story of Lucifer's refusal to bow down before newly created man, which is the Islamic version of the angelical fall, appears on the surface to be a justification of man's pride (since Lucifer, in so doing, disobeys the command of God). In fact, its meaning is the opposite of this. Iblis, who is Lucifer or (after his fall) Satan, represents the intellectual faculty in man, his highest function, which refuses to bow down before the "innermost heart of the Godhead" that is manifested in the human form. Paintings of this episode clarify its true interpretation. Man lies naked, prone upon the ground, surrounded by angels prostrating themselves at God's command, while Iblis-Lucifer sits proudly looking on. The whole scene is taking place within man's soul, where his highest faculty, the very one that is capable of bringing him into direct communion with the divinity within himself, rejects that communion by refusing to pay homage to that same divinity manifested in his outward shape — "a thing of clay," as the mighty Archangel scornfully protests. It is not man in his own right who is worthy of the angels' worship. When Blake wrote justly of "the human form divine," he was speaking of the outward manifestation of an implantation of the Word of God.

Julian, in her *Revelations*, says, "By Adam I understand All-Man." This is the accepted teaching of the three great religions — Judaism, Christianity, and Islam — that include in their scriptures the story of Adam and Eve ("the Adam") in the paradisal garden. *Kabbalah* explicitly teaches the androgyny of the original Adam; and this idea recurs frequently in all those interpretive writings that incline towards the more profound and esoteric aspects of the myth. Origen, the great Church Father who, in the third century A.D., conducted a school in Alexandria, and Philo, the Jewish neoplatonist, who taught in the same city, are but two of those who stressed the male-female nature of the all-containing archetypal man. This does not mean that the unified Adam was physically hermaphroditic; it means that his bodily form was, in some way that we cannot understand, not a perversion of nature but nature's fulfillment. Hinduism depicts the god Siva in a male-female shape, female on the left side, male on the right. This depiction is a symbolic representation of a mystery that cannot be visualized in terms of anything we know. The "great" Adam (called, in *Kabbalah*, Adam Kadmon) transcends and contains sexual polarity, as he transcends and contains all the burgeoning variety of the paradisal garden—which, as it comes into existence, appears as the exteriorization of himself. He—who is equally she—is prior to the rest of creation, according to the law whereby the greater, being nearer to God, precedes and breaks up into the lesser.

From this point of view, the account given in Genesis, where the garden and its creatures appear to precede the man and woman who are placed in their midst, will appear inexplicable until we realize that the process being described is here imagined as taking place *in time*, where nature forms the man from the child and the hen from the egg, and the eternal priorities appear in reverse. In this story, man has, as it were, *reappeared* in the center of his own unfolded image. Adam Kadmon has become the Adam or Adam and Eve. Duality, multiplicity, corporeality, and time have emerged from unity, but have not yet resulted in opposition. From the center which he occupies, man proceeds to give names to the various animal species who are the living symbols of his own functions and attributes. From that center he deviates, throwing all things out of balance, when he chooses to assert his own will against the will of God.

He falls, then, into the bonds of hostile nature and relentless time. In the paradisal garden, nature and time are a wholeness of beauty surpassing anything that we can now imagine, even in our dreams. The space-time continuum revolves in a blissful harmony corresponding to that within the soul of man himself. Always man's outer world must be the expression of his inward state. Falling into sin, he finds himself in a wasteland where nature and time have turned against him. Left to himself, he must perish. But God will follow him (fall with him) even to the world's end. As the myth unfolds, the place of Crucifixion is found to be the site of Adam's grave, the Tree of Death sprouts from the skull of sinful man, the Resurrection Garden is the New Eden, whose gardener is the Christ.[1]

A distinction has to be made between the wasteland of Genesis, where the ground brings forth thorns and thistles, and Adam at first has no prospect other than that of returning to the dust, and our own familiar world which is, as it were, a "half-way house." We ourselves are the Adam as we turn ourselves away from the wasteland of our sin by the saving action within us of the incarnating Christ, and begin our journey back; and so our world becomes the extension or reflection of our journeying state. God, in becoming man, enables man to be reborn in union with Himself; that is the meaning of the Christian myth. The Christ-in-us is both human and divine. If the Fathers of the Church spent a great deal of time splitting metaphysical hairs on the subject of what was known as the hypostatic union of the two natures in Christ, this was no mere theological game, but the necessary exercise of discovering who and what we really are. (Those of us who are unwilling to regard the Incarnation as "an historical event, taking place once and for all time in the person of Jesus, may consider the story unfolded in the gospels as a sort of 'model' to enable us to understand ourselves in our divine-human essentiality as sons of God. To repeat what has already been said, it is not of the essence of Christianity to regard the man Jesus as having been uniquely divine in the sense generally given to the Church's teaching on this subject. The idea of the transcendental unity of religions suggests rather that he was one of a predestined number of teachers of mankind who, understanding the Mystery at the root of our being, submerged their own personalities in the role of the God-man. His own statements, as recorded in the gospels, support this interpretation.)

"God became man that man might become God." This saying is attributed to so many of the early Fathers (Augustine, Athanasius, and Cyril of Jerusalem, to name but three) that it seems like the utterance of the Church itself. When all is said and done, we find that our merely human nature is something that we never experience as a simple state, because the state we are actually in is inevitably either higher or lower than it. Our human nature is an interface between the Divine-in-us and the for-us-unattainable innocence of the beasts. The Garden of Eden is a moment in and out of time. It has flown from our grasp; and now we cannot be as the unfallen Adam in that garden. We cannot, on the other hand, by sinking into an identification with our animal nature, be as the animals in their innocence. The choice is otherwise for us. We are called upon to choose between the pride of trying to be "as gods" and the way of obedience that will divinize our nothingness in Christ. If we choose wrongly, we may have the temporary illusion of being "as gods," but all the time we are sinking to a "bestial" level of which the animal world itself has no experience.

It is illuminating to consider the terms in which human beings insult one another. "You pig!" . . . "You cat!" . . . Scarcely any species of animal is not named in this way as a term of criticism and abuse. This is grievously unjust to the animals, who in no way merit such comparisons; yet there is a deep reason behind it. In the hierarchy of being, the human state is higher than the animal nature in which it participates. Therefore, when a human being forgets his humanity (as he does, in fact, every time he betrays the divinity which has been bestowed upon his humanity) and identifies himself with his animal nature, he displays the negative characteristics of that nature. Each species of animal, being contained within man, represents a particular function or virtue that is proper to man. But every one of our natural attributes has a positive and a negative aspect. The pig is not, of itself, a dirty, gross, bad-tempered creature. These characteristics are the reverse aspect of the virtues the pig was intended to express; they manifest themselves insofar as man, by stooping to the level of the pig, distorts its porcine nature, upsetting its equilibrium in such a way that its negativity is brought out. All that is negative and "bad" in the animal kingdom is made so by man; and this is so even where the animal in question has never been in physical contact with a man. Nature, including the animals, was torn from its paradise by Adam's sin; yet still it retains its primal innocence, holding itself in a balance which it continuously readjusts. Man's very existence in this world depends upon the holding of this balance. All the processes of nature, including natural disasters, storms, and earthquakes, as well as those great annual, lunar, and diurnal rhythms that contain our lives, assist in holding it. In return, in his own long process of return, man carries nature with him, back into the heart of God. That is the meaning of the Bodhisattva vow: "I will not enter Nirvana till every living being can enter with me." As Meister Eckhart wrote, "The soul never rests till she is gotten into God who is the first form, and creatures never rest till they have gotten into human nature: therein do they attain to their original form, God namely."

Man contains all things. This Mystery is a commonplace of the Wisdom literature of every time and place.

> Man contains all that is above in heaven and below upon earth, the celestial as well as the terrestrial creatures . . . No world could exist before Adam came into being, for the human figure contains all things, and all that is exists by virtue of it.
>
> *Zohar* or *Book of Splendor*
> (Thirteenth-century Spanish, part of Kabbalah)

> One man is equivalent to all creation. One man is a World in miniature.
>
> Abot de Rabbi Nathan
> Second Century

> O God! In Thy body I see all the gods, as well as multitudes of all kinds of beings.
>
> *Bhagavad Gita*
> Arjuna address Krishna, the Divine Man

> Man is in a manner all creatures.
>
> St. Gregory the Great

> Man is the microcosm in the strictest sense of the word. He is the summary of all existence. There is no creature that is not recapitulated in man.
>
> John Scotus Erigena
> Ninth-century Christian theologian

> It is a great truth which you should seriously consider, that there is nothing in heaven or upon earth which does not also exist in Man . . .
>
> Paracelsus
> Sixteenth-century Swiss alchemist

> All creatures that have flowed out from God must become united into one Man.
>
> Meister Eckhart

This teaching refers not only to earthly creatures, but to the angels of heaven, those thoughts in the mind of God that become embodied in the temporal world, blindingly beautiful archetypal beings ordered in a majestic hierarchy that extends from the seraphim and cherubim about the throne to the multitude of guardians who fly between heaven and earth. The angels are both within man and above him. They are within him as the components of his hidden perfection, above him as representing the perfection he has yet to attain. The great symbol of the Blessed Virgin's Assumption into heaven, her body together with her soul borne upwards by adoring angels, represents the culmination of our human destiny, when the body of this world is made one with the Divine Thought, and all the unthinkably beautiful components of that thought move towards its total manifestation at the end of time.

It is said of man, in the holy Qur'an, "His are the keys of the heavens and the earth." As the First Man (Adam) named all things as they passed before him in the garden, so the Last Man (Christ) will bestow upon each individual human soul a new name as it passes before Him into heaven, bearing with it those lesser creatures for whom it has been responsible in this world. So man holds the "keys" for all creatures; hence the symbol of the crossed keys pertaining to the Pope of Rome, himself a symbol of the one man who, at the zenith of all worlds, awaits his divinization in the Christ.

It is frequently implied that the lower worlds progressively die into one another until they attain the human state. Rumi expresses the idea of the human monad rising upwards through the realms into which it has fallen, bringing salvation to those worlds in the course of its ascent:

> I died as mineral and became a plant,
> I died as plant and rose to animal,
> I died as animal and I was Man.
> Why should I fear? When was I less by dying?

Yet once more I shall die as Man, to soar
With angels blest; but even from angelhood
I must pass on: all except God doth perish...

Mythological stones, plants, and animals appear in all traditions. Christ Himself is called the Lamb of God, because the lamb typifies purity and innocence laid upon the altar of sacrifice. The lion, most superbly beautiful of all creatures, has been widely regarded as the king of beasts, while the dog has been despised as the lowliest and dirtiest of animals. Yet, paradoxically, it is the dog that has been more nearly humanized than any other species, an example of the saying that the last shall be first, which is one of the root ideas of the Christian tradition. The ass that looked down into the manger, and carried the Christ into the city where He was to encounter death, is man's corporal nature. And so on... remembering always that these are not "invented" symbols, but inspired interpretations of the true meaning of the species in question. Perhaps the most mysterious of all the lower creation is the monkey, who, whether or not he was our ancestor in the temporal world, stands for our animal nature, the highest point that could be reached along a certain line before humanity could be attained. Humanity implies a spiritual descent from higher worlds, a meeting place between that which comes down from heaven and that which has been raised up slowly from the depths. The monkey represents the point at which the line divides; it stays behind, the sadness in its eyes reminding us of what might have been. There is a horrid significance in the fact that in this age of man's Promethean pride, it is monkeys who are tortured more than any other beast, in the interests of controlling human minds and "conquering" space. But the monkey in us will follow us to the end, and be with us in God.

Man, the Androgyn, fell (we are told in the myth) into a deep sleep, in which his God-reflecting unity was divided, and he became two. This was the moment "before" the breaking up of the primal creation (man himself) into multiplicity. It represents the first division.

The constantly changing relationships between the sexes that occur in traditional mythology produce shifting patterns of such complexity that no one who has not been granted a special vocation to do so should attempt to unravel them. The time is overdue for a radical re-examination of this whole vast subject by spiritually and intellectually qualified theologians within the Church. Never has such a re-examination been more needed; never has it been more unlikely to take place. The Church has apparently forgotten its metaphysics. Yet the problems associated with human sexuality have their roots in the most profound metaphysical considerations. Doctrines such as the Immaculate Conception of the Virgin and her Assumption into heaven, the very ones that are most obviously relevant to these considerations, are being discounted and regarded with embarrassment. In this situation one is in a quandary. For most of us, advanced metaphysical studies are desirable only insofar as they are individually needed for the correction of distortions or the clarification of bewilderment. There is a sort of intellectual promiscuity that can blur the pristine clarity of a childlike mind—and the mind must remain childlike, no matter how far it extends itself. On the other hand, in the present climate of superficiality, when all and sundry are expressing opinions without recourse to the only kind of knowledge that can bring enlightenment, whoever craves truth must push his or her understanding to its limits in order to find it. Unaided by the teaching authority that should be, but is not, provided by the present-day Church, we must gaze into unfathomable mysteries in order to fish out from their depths a few elementary principles by which to live.

A hierarchical arrangement of function will be found to be a constant characteristic of the world of sacred myth. (This idea is in no way inconsistent with that of the equality of souls before God, or of persons, as such, in the context of a personal relationship or a gathering of friends.) All things proceed from and return to the One, in a pattern which reflects itself in the forms and functions of all living beings, mythology being simply a way of compressing into linear stories various aspects of this pattern—which exists as a metaphysical reality behind whatever traditional imagery may be employed to express it. This pattern requires constantly to be real-ized. Thus the myths and rituals of a given religion will reappear in the social structures and customs of the society for which that religion provides the foundation. All things will be ordered to produce a strict correspondence between the hidden reality, the mythology, the religious practices, the social organization, and the natural characteristics of the environment. This is the meaning of order; and if order is not maintained, there will be a falling apart from the center and the whole structure will disintegrate. As widely as the religious and social patterns of human collectivities may differ in their outward forms, they must all, to survive, obey certain universal laws. One of these laws is that of correspondences, above described; another is that whereby a central symbol stands for the metaphysical Unity upon which all else depends. For this Unity we use the code word "God"; and its primary symbol will always be a man, the "Perfect Man."

The Perfect Man (the Christ) is a Reality for whom a number of mythical figures and a number of actual individuals can stand proxy, as symbols of that Reality, in those times and places for which their appearance is appropriate. Jesus stands as one such proxy, as does

Muhammad. So also does every king, every father of a family, every parish priest. There is no end to the ceaselessly multiplying circles, generating outwards to infinity, each one of which requires a coordinating principle to align it to the greater circles, which in turn align it to the One. To these symbols, these proxies, we owe reverence, and that reverence increases, the nearer the proxy stands to that which it represents. By such means are we required to direct our worship. They lead us, through the Perfect Man, to God. And if we say that beyond even the Divine Unity is the namelessness of the ineffable Godhead, the AYIN in whose depths the mystic aspires to be lost, this does not release us from the obligation to prostrate ourselves before the One, the AIN SOF that includes all being in itself. The idea that any traditional society has ever been, or ever could be, "polytheistic" is a misunderstanding arising out of ignorance. The "gods" of the so-called "polytheistic" religions may be seen as attributes, modes or functions of the One, whose centrality is implied or, more often, explicitly defined. In Christianity, these attributes are represented by the angels and the major saints. The twelve apostles encircle the figure of Christ. In a further expansion of the image, each member of the original "foundation" becomes the "head" of a subordinate collectivity extending outwards in the same way to become the Church.

According to the ancient wisdom, number (understood in a sense no longer dreamed of in mathematics) expresses the foundation-pattern of the cosmos. From the idea of a descending hierarchy, expressible in terms of number, we come back to that of the original dyad without which there can be no existence, but which, being in itself the number of opposition, must instantaneously produce the reconciling third in order to avoid creating and perpetuating strife. There is no existent phenomenon that does not imply and necessitate its opposite. Behind existence, there remains the

One, the AIN SOF of *Kabbalah*, the Self of *Vedanta*, the unity of the three-in-one of the Christian Trinity. Islam affirms continuously that God is one. But from one must proceed two, before three can complete the basic pattern in the new unity of love which issues in the first creative act. Human sexuality corresponds to this necessary principle of opposition. Its twin polarities, male and female, are equal only as they remain in opposition. In their reconcilement, they cannot be so; insofar as there must always be a "one" to stand proxy for the one in every situation that reflects the order of the trinitarian God. (In the Mystery of the Holy Trinity itself, God the Father represents the one, which is why the Orthodox Church jealously affirms His superiority by its rejection of the "filoque clause,"[2] while the other Churches stress the equality of the three persons by retaining that clause.) In the Christian system, the female principle is subordinate, which is not to say that women are subordinate to men, since every individual human being is male-female in a body that manifests, and performs the functions of, one or other of the two. The specifically male functions are determined by the fact that the male body is the primary image of androgynous man, while the female body derives from that image and is contained therein (an idea which finds expression in the story of Eve emerging from the body of Adam while he slept). It is for this reason that Christian symbolism excludes the idea of women priests. A priest is the representative of Christ; and the male body represents upon earth the full manhood (male-female) as it is in Christ. Into that fullness, in the Mystery of the Assumption of the Virgin and her Coronation in heaven, the Femininity returns.[3]

Christianity expresses, in terms of its own symbolism, universal laws that are the same in all times and places, wherever we look. Those mythological systems that are centered upon the Great Goddess, the Earth Mother, who dominates and slays her consort (who may also be her brother, and is frequently reborn as her son) are not "untrue" in relation to the higher religions; they are merely incomplete. They stop short at nature worship; except in those cases where there is a progression from the first pair and the continuous cycle of growth, disappearance, and return, to the greater Mystery of the eternally risen and triumphant God. (In ancient Egypt, for instance, the Second Horus typified such a progression.) The Great Goddess is the personification of nature, whose powers of creation and destruction are held in a continuously alternating balance. Her male partner, though a god, is inferior to herself. (From one level of being to the next, hierarchical positions are reversed: thus in nature the female principle is ascendant.) The death (at her hands, or at least at her instigation) of her spouse will be repeated over and over again, corresponding as it does to the rhythms of summer and winter, day and night. Early rites of the vernal equinox reveal her in this role. In India she is Kali, the Black One, most fearful of all imaginable divinities: yet in no one of her many appearances is she to be understood as a personification of malevolence. Always she is the holy one, the servant of necessity. So how are we to interpret her in relation to the Virgin of the Christian myth—and what does she tell us of the meaning of womanhood in our own lives, so that we may begin to untangle the vast confusions surrounding this subject at the present time?

She tells us that wherever she, the female principle, is worshipped as preeminent, the male—now envisaged as her dyadic opposite, not as the higher principle to which she will be united in her final state—becomes a depleted shadow of what, in the Christian system, is meant by man as the representative on earth of the creator God. Man either contains woman or is less than woman. In a female-orientated system the male principle is reduced to that which must periodically die in its opposite and be reborn and die once more. Prisoned forever in the trap of time, this being can save neither the woman nor himself. His female partner, powerful and dominant as she may be, is trapped in ambiguity, compelled, as Nature is compelled, to be the taker of the life she gives. Only the Perfect Man provides an unambiguous interface between the world and God. The Virgin Mary is unambiguous; but she is not, in herself, divine; neither is she, by herself, complete. Even in her heavenly state, she is but the perfected femininity reabsorbed into the divine-human Androgyn who is the Christ.

Nature may be, under God, adored; but she may not be worshipped. Her powers may not be used, save insofar as they have been bestowed upon the user by the grace of God in Christ.[4] Present-day "witch cults," associated with the Women's Movement, may protest their benignity, but of their very nature they are double-edged. Christianity has, as we shall see, its "dark goddess," whose feet may be embraced by the penitent, but her Mystery is a turning of her previous triumphs inside out.

8

Reality or Illusion?

"The world has become a man, and man a world," wrote the Persian Sufi, Shabistari (d. 1320 A.D.). Modern quantum physics has begun, haltingly, to rediscover what our forefathers were taught more clearly and were able to receive with less bewilderment. Shabistari says of man:

He is at once seen, seeing eye, and thing seen.
The holy tradition hath declared this.

We live in a world that appears to be as it appears to be by our common consent. Even from one period of time to another, from one part of the globe to another, our world adjusts itself obediently to our vision. (Homer would have us believe that he saw a "wine dark sea"; is this a poetic convention, or did the sea itself appear in a different light, all those centuries ago in ancient Greece?) The thought is intensely disturbing to those scientifically conscious men and women in the world today who are only now beginning to realize, with incredulity, what they are actually being told by the science they have put into the place of authority vacated by the Church. There is, however, one absolutely fundamental difference between traditional mysticism and modern physics, which lies in the inability of the latter to discover an objective reality behind the shifting veils of the subject-object relationship. The scientific method cannot, of its very nature, proceed beyond the limitations of phenomenal existence. It can do this no more than we, in our earthly bodies, can travel faster than the speed of light. Religious tradition, enlightened from above downwards, presents a divine revelation as the necessary framework within which to place the findings of a science that proceeds from the physical world upwards, until it reaches the outermost barriers of space-time—where it is suddenly brought to a standstill in great astonishment.

"What is worship?" asks the Sufi mystic Ansari (d. 1088 A.D.); and answers his own question: "To real-ize reality." There is still the suggestion of a subject-object relationship. But now there is an obligation laid upon the subject to identify himself with the objectively real and, in so doing, bring into existence in space-time a reality that forever *is*, and in itself transcends space-time.

> All forms of being in the corporal world are images of pure Lights, which exist in the spiritual world.
> Suhrawardi
> Twelfth-century founder of
> an order of Sufis in Baghdad

> Know that all the shapes and images which you see with your bodily eyes in the world of things that come to be and cease to be are mere semblances and copies of the forms which have real existence in the thought-world, those forms which are eternal and will never cease to be.

Hermes Trismegistus
Author of a body of mystical
writings much revered in the
Middle Ages, whose name is
lost to history

To thy care the figur'd seals consigned
Which stamp the world with forms of ev'ry kind.
                    Orphic Hymn (c. 500 B.C.)

It is that reassurance of a reality beyond our subjective experience that no scientist, as such, is in a position to hold out to us, because it is not, and will never be, within the reach of any human science. Those who are eager to foist upon us the notion that the great sages of the East were picturesque forerunners of our contemporary physicists, presenting the same world view couched in the language of myth, are blind leaders of the blind. What they are saying is a half-truth, and a dangerously misleading one at that. "Hindu mythology," writes one of them, "is virtually a large-scale projection into the psychological realm of microscopic scientific discoveries. Hindu deities such as Shiva and Vishnu continually dance the creation and destruction of universes, while the Buddhist image of the wheel of life symbolizes the unending process of birth, death, and rebirth which is a part of the world of form, which is emptiness, which is form."[1] Maybe. But undreamed of in this new philosophy is the "Unbecome, Unborn, Unmade, Unformed" that bestows reality and eternity upon all that is become, born, made, and formed; Hinduism's moveless One behind the ceaseless dancing of its lesser gods; the Tao that cannot be named of the *Tao Te Ching*:

The Tao that can be told is not the eternal Tao.
The name that can be named is not the eternal name.
The nameless is the beginning of heaven and earth.

What can the science of the physical world know of the Lord of the Shvetashvatara Upanishad?

> O Lord who has woven the web of the world from
> thyself, as a spider spins its threads,
> Lead us to Brahman.

Lead us . . . for we are not qualified to lead ourselves. Nothing could be more dangerous than the prospect typically suggested by Professor G. F. Chew, Chairman of the Physics Department at Berkeley, when he writes that we are on the verge of "a completely new form of human intellectual endeavor, one that will not only lie outside physics but will not even be describable as 'scientific.'."[2]

It is one thing for our science to extend itself to its limits; quite another to aspire to pass beyond those limits in some new way that bypasses the way of faith. In the *Tao Te Ching* it is written that we come to a place where there is

> darkness within darkness
> the gate to all mystery.

Our physicists and astro-physicists have arrived at that place. Let them stop there and keep silence. Let them wait.

And after all it was not only the Hindus and the Buddhists who anticipated what we are now being told about wave formations that appear as we look for them. Fifteen centuries ago St. Augustine wrote of those formations, but without being misled into supposing that we and they are caught forever in a subject-object trap: "Gaze at the sky, the earth, the sea, and all the things that shine in them or above them, or creep or fly or swim beneath them. They have forms because they have rhythm; take this away, and they will no longer be. From whom are they, save from Him, from whom rhythm is . . ."

The Sanskrit word is *Maya*. It is often translated as "illusion," but it meant originally "the power to divide," implying that the world of appearances proceeds from the act of division, whereby the many are made to emerge from the One; so that Maya is the manifoldness of things, which is indeed illusion but also the means whereby God manifests Himself. The mother of the Buddha—who, like the Blessed Virgin, conceived by an angelical visitation—is called Maya, because she was the instrument of a divine manifestation. Maya is both veil *and* manifestation, illusion *and* a semblance of reality. The following passage from the writings of the Master known as "Hermes Trismegistus" elucidates the paradox: "This world rightly regarded is a place for learning truth in. The visible forms of things which it presents to our senses are fleeting and perishable; but they are semblances or shadows of forms that are not apprehensible by sense, forms that are real and everlasting."

The Sufi Ibn Farid leads us further into the same thought:

> Existence is a veil in the beginning of the mystic life, and also in its middle stage, but not in its end. [In its end] God reveals Himself to the mystic in both His aspects at once, so that he sees with his bodily eye the beauty of the Divine Essence manifested under the attribute of the Outward.

Maya—the appearance of things—reveals the Divine Beauty.

> The real orchards and fruits are in the heart:
> the reflexion of their beauty is falling upon this water
> and earth.
>
> Rumi

St. Bernard, as he passed through a fair landscape, drew his cowl over his face. Those who see traces of God in the beauties of nature find this hard to understand. Only the achievement of perfect purity of heart will resolve the contradiction and solve the problem.

> The glass grows clear
>   the wine grows clear;
> one resembles another,
>   all is confused
> as if there were wine and no cup . . .
> or cup
>   and no wine.
>   Sahib ibn 'Abbad

St. John of the Cross was, supremely, the mystic of Divine Darkness, poet of the way of the negation of images, yet he puts into the mouth of Nature, in answer to the soul who inquires of her if the Beloved has passed by, these words:

> Rare gifts he scattered
> As through the woods and groves he pass'd apace,
> Turning, as on he sped,
> And clothing every place
> With loveliest reflection of his face.

Dionysius writes of the "Creative Cause" that it "holds all things in existence by their yearning for their own Beauty." This links the idea of beauty with that of reality, implying that in reality only the beautiful exists. Insofar as this world is beautiful, it is real. And it is beautiful insofar as we see it as being so (which does not mean that we should close our eyes to the evil that has come into the world, but that we should so purify ourselves that we see through the evil, permitting it to pass through us without resistance). This world, the product of our common vision, would become the Garden of Paradise if we were all of us in a state of innocence: as things are, even the saints cannot see it as other than a place of suffering, even while they glimpse its pristine loveliness in every natural form that has been permitted to remain unspoiled. Individual moments of vision have the quality of memory. As Rumi expresses it in the poem which his translator calls "Remembered Music":

> We, who are parts of Adam, heard with him
> The song of angels and of seraphim.
> Our memory, though dull and sad, retains
> Some echo still of those unearthly strains.

The Garden of Paradise is the world's beginning, not its end. The experience of the saints breaks through even the most beautiful of passing forms and turns the world towards heaven, our final state. The Garden was a flash of innocence in the first instant of time, before pollution came. The saints see beyond time. They see into the final metamorphosis of all the things that are. That is the reality of our world. We shall see it when we are able to endure it, not that we shall have created it by seeing it, for it is always here; but that we, by submitting ourselves to it, shall have made it real in us. Whatever is to be the culmination of the history of our world-in-time, this ultimate consummation will not fail to come about.

A sublimely beautiful poem of the early centuries A.D., generally described as "gnostic," but resembling in many respects the parable of the Prodigal Son, teaches us the unwisdom of defining "this world" as being in itself either "bad" or "good." Known as the *Hymn of the Pearl*, it appears at first glance to describe the human soul in exile in a world of sin; but a deeper interpretation reveals a greater complexity. We begin to see how our way of experiencing our world-in-time causes it to reflect back to us first one and then another of our states of mind. For the changes of place which the poem describes are in reality changes of state.

A king's son is sent by his father into the land of Egypt to bring back "one pearl which is in the midst of the sea in the abode of the loud-breathing serpent." "Egypt" has the same meaning here as in the stories of the flight of the Holy Family from the wrath of Herod, and of Joseph in the Old Testament. The place of exile is at the same time the place of hiding. In Egypt the young prince conceals himself "in garments like theirs." He does not wish to be recognized "as an alien." This is a subtle and complex idea not to be interpreted merely as the cowardice of a weak spirit. The Holy Child Himself was hidden in Egypt. We hide ourselves in darkness because we are not yet ready for the sacrifice we shall eventually be called upon to make. We fall asleep in time, which is itself a kind of sleep. In the *Hymn of the Pearl*, the King and Queen send a message to their son: "Up and arise from thy sleep . . . remember the pearl . . ." The pearl, like the grain of mustard seed and the treasure hid in a field, represents the divine image in the heart of man.

> I remembered the pearl . . .
> And I began to charm him,
> The terrible loud-breathing serpent,
> I hushed him to sleep and I lulled him into slumber,
> For my Father's name I named over him
> And I snatched away the pearl
> And turned to go back

His "bright robe," which he had left behind in his father's kingdom, is sent to meet him, and he recognizes it as his own.

On a sudden as I faced it,
The garment seemed to me like a mirror of myself.
I saw it in my whole self,
Moreover I faced my whole self in facing it
For we were two in distinction
And yet again one in likeness. . .

The robe is described in all its dazzling beauty.

And in the hands of its givers
It hastened that I might take it.
For me too my love urged me on
That I should run to meet it and receive it,
And I stretched forth and received it,
With the beauty of its colors I adorned myself. . .

He returns to his father, the king, who rejoices over him.

And I was with him in his kingdom. . .
And he promised that also to the gate
Of the King of Kings I should speed with him,
And bringing my gift and my pearl
I should appear with him before our King.

After all, there is another and a higher King, beyond the father of the prince. The hierarchies continuously ascend, with every central figure directing the attention of the group surrounding it to the one above.

The whole of this poem is an image of our world as we experience it in time: place of exile, of pilgrimage, of hiding, way out, way back. The soul travels in a spiral of time, spirals within spirals, in search of a "pearl," until in the end it is reunited with its true self. There is no one way of thinking about our world. It is a darksome prison while we submit to self-imprisonment; but when we set out upon the way of return it becomes a winding path of light.

9

How Can A Man
Be Born Again?

The "bright robe" of pure light in the *Hymn of the Pearl* is the garment of the reborn. It represents the true self that remained behind in God when the merely human will, the ego or me-consciousness, fell into sin. Its dazzling colors are those of white light seen through a prism. White, which is a constantly recurring symbol in the Christian tradition, must always, within that tradition, be understood in its positive sense, not as the absence of color but as the totality of all colors. In the white baptismal robe the colors are quiescent, as it were, asleep, waiting to blaze forth when the newborn soul has grown to its full stature as a type of Christ. The white robes of the saints in heaven are of another sort, blindingly luminous, with all the colors of the spectrum vibrantly awake, oned in a radiance never seen upon this earth.

Jesus told Nicodemus, "Except a man be born again he shall not see the Kingdom of God." Nicodemus, troubled by the obvious impossibility of a man being "born when he is old," questions how this can be. He receives no explanation, apart from being told that he is thinking in terms of the flesh, whereas "that which is born of the spirit is Spirit." Rebirth in the Spirit, then, is a precondition of entry into the kingdom. Our Christ-being must be born in us, to enable us to be reborn in it. It must become adult in us, and carry us with it, through the Cross of sacrifice, into the Resurrection and the heavenly state. The birth of Christ in me, and mine in Him, are one event. That event is a double baptism, by water (which brings about purification) and the Spirit (which burns away the lower self). The rite of baptism, as administered by the Church, is the formal representation of an operation within the soul, whereby the divine spark of its creation, having been once denied, is re-introduced. In a timeless instant the soul is misled by the ego-consciousness to deny its God. In that same instant God recaptures it and causes it to be reborn. The Church of England has described baptism as "the outward and visible sign of an inward and spiritual grace." Obviously the grace is not confined to those who have outwardly been baptized, but we should not deduce from this that the sacrament is not, in itself, precisely what it is believed to be: the sacrament co-inheres in the operation; as the operation, whenever and wherever it takes place, co-inheres in the sacrament.

The entire cycle of the Christian myth centers upon the Mystery of the soul's passage through the whorls of time, from its beginnings in the formless dark, illumined by the tiny Christ-spark in the innermost sanctuary of the self. The myth has been seen by more than a few of the saints as the prototype of all romance. St. John of the Cross wrote a cycle of poems entitled *Romance*, beginning with a definition in verse of the love within the Holy Trinity, and culminating in a description of the Nativity, in which the Holy Babe is laid in the manger together with his Beloved, the human soul. Angelus Silesius, who was in the

habit of expressing the most exalted contemplations in the
form of little rhymes, produced this naive exclamation of
childlike happiness and triumph:

> The angels are in bliss but better is man's life for no
> one of their kind can ever be God's wife!

God's "wife" is also his daughter and his mother in the
sacred myth. Sophia, the daughter, enters this world as
Mary, who gives birth to the Holy Child. This birth of
the divine spark within the soul can take place only when
the soul-center has been made pure by its coincidence with
the principle of purity represented by the Mother of God.
The Virgin Mary is the one human being whose soul-
substance is a spotless mirror unresistant to the heavenly
light. (This doctrine of the Immaculate Conception is
frequently confused by non-Catholics with the Virgin birth,
thus misleading them into supposing that it implies the
"sinfulness" of sex.) Conversely, she is herself the still
untarnished center of the soul, as Julian saw it in her vision
of the "little child" who "swiftly glided up into heaven."
But Mary of the Immaculate Conception is clothed in a
perfection that is not yet that of the Virgin of the
Assumption, Bride of God. The mystical marriage is
accomplished only as the Bride is reunited with her pilgrim-
self (the repentant Magdalen of the myth) and with that
which is the pure negation of herself, the Negative
Femininity that appears in the Christian Mystery as the
Cross. From this reunion there comes into being a new
cycle of time, a new manifestation of the Son.

"Woman, behold thy son." Among the innermost
"secrets" of Christian esotericism is the idea, constantly
implied, if seldom made explicit, that St. John the Beloved
will be the "next" manifestation of the Christ, appearing
in the "next" great cycle of time that unfolds from the Last

Day when the pilgrim souls of the present cycle will be judged. The symbol of the eagle of St. John, rising from the chalice of the Last Supper, while St. John himself lies asleep across the bosom of the Son, in total identification with the sacrificial act, signifies the birth that is to come, emergent from the *Vas Spiritualis,* the womb of the Mother of God.[1] And while it is not always wise to strain our minds so far beyond their tiny scope, the implication is that every human soul must one day play the part of John. One whole great cycle of time belongs to everyone who bears upon his heart the sign of Christ.

The Feast of the Nativity celebrates the coming into being of a point of light. The point will expand infinitely to become a globe, the heavenly sun or Son. (The play on words is felicitous; esoteric teachings frequently make use of puns, word games, cryptograms, and the like.) Now we are in the realm of many dimensions, and cannot see how it is that the globe is moving from within, forever returning upon itself and once more opening out. Christ's natal point coincides with that of his conception (in the Mystery of the Annunciation), death, and rising from the dead. In the myth the Nativity is linked to the Resurrection by the parallel stories of the two Josephs: the one who surrendered the virgin womb of his newly wedded wife; the other who gave up the new tomb he had purchased for himself, to receive the body of the Son of God. If the scene of the Nativity is adorned with a more lavish wealth of symbolism than that surrounding the greater of the two events, the reason is that the nearer one approaches the central Mystery, the simpler and more unified the encircling images become. At Easter, the risen Christ steps out into a burgeoning garden, the regenerated paradise. The light of the heavenly sun has taken possession of the earth.

The feast of the birth of Divine Light in human darkness was not invented by the Church. It is older than history, occurring always at the winter solstice, when the sun is at its nadir, the night is black, and all the world is wrapped in silence. This darkness is not to be understood as an evil influence. It is the condition of creation. The human soul, called out of the nadir of nonbeing, aspires towards the light; but that nadir is God in his mode of Divine Darkness: some, at least, of the mystics have declared that it is the Divine Ipseity itself. Darkness only becomes menacing and filled with illusions of evil when the soul asserts the self-sufficiency of itself by-itself. Otherwise, as Islam declares of its own most sacred moment, when, on the Night of Power, the Prophet received the ultimate revelation before the throne of God: "That night is peace till break of dawn. . . ."

One of the more esoteric and inaccessible figures associated with the Nativity is that of the first St. John. His connection with the Beloved Disciple is apparent from the identity of name and the placing of the two feasts at, respectively, the summer and the winter solstices. Both are the sons of Mary in a certain sense: The second becomes so at the foot of the Cross; the first appears in this character in countless traditional paintings showing Mary alone with the two children — or, in a few instances (notably in the famous Leonardo cartoon), accompanied by a grand-motherly figure, described as St. Anne but resembling a Demeter-like goddess in possession of eternal youth. The two old women, St. Anne and the Baptist's mother, St. Elizabeth, tend to be merged together alike in Christian iconography and in the myth. Their stories are nearly identical; and a number of parallels can be traced between these two stories and those of the great earth goddesses of earlier times. The child St. John appears, almost invariably, in the act of offering something to the infant Christ. This may be a bird or a lamb, flowers, a twist of corn, a fruit for Him to eat. He is sturdy and strong, while the Christ Child is wistful and delicate. One is led to conclude that St. John is the merely human or natural counterpart of the Holy Child, as it were the interface on the side of nature in its meeting with God's Son. "And whence is this to me that the mother of my Lord should come to me!" cries Demeter-Elizabeth; and the babe leaps in her womb, quickened to spiritual life by this encounter with its heavenly twin. In earthly terms the "twin" is the younger of the two by six months. Nature is "older" than the presence of God in nature, in the sense that the Word must descend into an already prepared environment. As might be expected, the relationship is not without a number of mythological precedents. In the temple art of ancient Egypt, the Divine Horus is depicted in the company of his twin, a pairing believed to represent the higher (Divine) and the lower (human) KA.

St. John offers his "cousin" the fruits of nature. Later he will offer Him the baptism of nature—water, nature's purification, which calls down the Spirit by the attraction of its own reflection in the watery depths. Of this baptism he declares to the people: "I indeed baptize you with water unto repentance: but he that cometh after me...shall baptize you with the Holy Ghost and with fire." Christian iconography depicts the Baptist in the act of pouring water on the head of Jesus while the Holy Ghost descends from Heaven. All the levels of being are drawn together in this operation, which is reproduced in the sacrament of baptism as administered by the Church. These levels have been variously classified; what is important to remember is that the beings of one level may be drawn upwards by the power of descending love, or driven downwards by the dragging tendency of sin. Man is a spiritual being (that is to say, he belongs, of his own nature, to a level that is not yet divine; neither is it merely "psychic") who must choose between being raised up into heaven or dragged down into the animal nature, which he should be drawing back into himself with the object of returning it to God. The animals have an intense psychic life of their own, which is capable of being spiritualized by man. In plants the psyche seems to dream; but under the care of a loving gardener it becomes vibrant. So through the whole chain of existence flows an aspiration; and from man, who alone is responsible for sin, a tendency to fall beneath materiality's oppressive weight. Baptism is the removal of that weight. It signifies the raising up of all beings (from the depths of the purifying water) in response to the divine descent.

Water is the great conductor. It cleanses at the same time as it regenerates. A fifth-century Nestorian homily on baptism declares that "the power of the Divinity dwells in the visible waters." It is as if this mysterious element sweeps in a great circle through earth and heaven, alternating back and forth from a spiritual to a physical substance, bearing with it both the grace of heaven and earth's physical and psychical excrement. So Rumi describes it:

> There is a Water that flows down from Heaven
> To cleanse the world from sin by grace Divine.
> At last, its whole stock spent, its virtue gone,
> Dark with pollution not its own, it speeds
> Back to the Fountain of all purities;
> Whence, freshly bathed, earthward it sweeps again,
> Trailing a robe of glory bright and pure.
> This Water is the Spirit of the Saints,
> Which ever sheds, until itself is beggared,
> God's balm on the sick soul; and then returns
> To Him who made the purest light of Heaven.

As it is the tears of Isis and Nepthys that regenerate the dead Osiris, so it is with Christ; his mother and the Magdalen weep over his body before confining it to the

tomb from which, after three days, it will rise again. The
tears of the Virgin have always been venerated by Catholics
as having the power to regenerate. They are seen to flow
miraculously from certain favored statues; paintings depict
them as rolling in great droplets down her cheeks. The
Nestorian homily already quoted sums up what was, by
the early fifth century, the symbolism commonly attached
to the waters of baptism, connecting them with the rites
of death:

> In the grave of the waters the priest buries the whole
> man; and he resuscitates him by the power of life that
> is hidden in his words. In the door of the tomb of
> baptism he stands equipped, and he performs there a
> mystery of death and of the resurrection. With the voice
> openly he preaches the power of what he is doing—
> how it is that a man dies in the water, and turns and
> lives again. He reveals and shows to him in whose name
> it is that he is to die and swiftly come to life.

One is reminded of the simulated death that was part
of the initiation ceremonies of the ancient Mysteries, which
exercised so potent an influence upon the early Church.
The Neoplatonic Christians of Alexandria deliberately
associated the Christian sacraments with those earlier rites:

> O eternally sacred Mysteries! The Lord is the high priest;
> he imprinted his seal on the Mystic when he granted
> him enlightenment; he places those who are believers
> and remain eternally in his care, in the hands of his
> Father. See here the spiritual ecstasy of our Mysteries,
> if you will. Be initiated and you will dance in the chorus
> of Angels, around the uncreated God, the Undying, the
> only true Being, while the divine Logos sings the holy
> hymn with us.
>
> Clement of Alexandria
> Third-century Greek theologian

Concurrently with the great flowering of mystical wisdom in that city, Christian baptism, which had previously been a simple ceremony, began to be surrounded by an elaborately solemn ritual, designed to impress upon the catechumen the idea that he was indeed being reborn, "by water and the Spirit," into a new world, the world of the coinherence of all souls in the Body of Christ, which is the Church. Sadly, although perhaps inevitably, it has proved to be impossible, in the course of history, for Christians to sustain the idea that a sacrament can be valid by its participation in the reality expressed in its symbolism, without being exclusive in the sense of the symbolism being essential to the actualization of that reality. The balance of the paradox is precarious. *Extra ecclesiam nulla salus*: those dreadful words, resulting not only in the dismissal of all other religions as "untrue," but in the casting out of "heretics" and the "unrepentant" by excommunication, into what was assumed to be the jaws of hell—mystically understood, are no more than the truth. Literally interpreted, as they have been, one can hardly wonder at the reaction which has rejected them together with their true meaning. The Church as an earthly institution will not survive unless it returns to an understanding of its own symbolism, without being misled into supposing that the outward sign is either necessary to the inward grace or automatically brings it about.

10

Why Suffering?

Rebirth is through suffering, sacrifice, and death.

We do not like this idea. At the present time it is rejected even by the Churches, where there is a sort of conspiracy to avoid the question of what has to happen before we begin to celebrate the risen life.

Jesus said, " . . . it must needs be that offences come; but woe to that man by whom the offence cometh." This is a strange saying, which may seem to us unjust; but its truth forces itself upon us. No one of us save by suffering may return to God. Yet I may not inflict suffering upon my neighbor, nor even (save in exceptional circumstances) seek it deliberately for myself. Death is the gateway to life. Yet I must not bring about another's death; and while I may sacrifice my life for another, I may not take it, or allow it to be taken, for my own sake. This is the law; and it runs through all the great traditions.(Perversions, resulting from the violent distortion of a truth, are liable to occur at any time. The Inquisition, the practice of *sati*, the protest-suicides of Buddhist monks, are only some of the horrors that have come about as a result of misunderstanding the idea of sacrifice.) Love does not inflict suffering; and it is required of us that we should practice love. Suffering, *all* suffering, was and is brought about by sin. Nevertheless, it is being used by the mercy of God as the means of releasing us from sin. Suffering is a transformative agent.

"It is sooth," Julian was told in one of her "shewings," "that sin is cause of all this pain; but all shall be well, and all manner of thing shall be well." Again and again she reassures us that there is "a marvellous high mystery," "a Great Deed that our Lord shall do," which when we see it, shall cause us to understand "that all-thing is done as it was then ordained before that anything was made." But to believe this, in the face of the world's suffering, is possible only for those who have a timeless perspective, who see clearly what it means to deny God for the sake of self. Before time began each one of us coinhered in that act whereby the principle of evil was let loose. No one of the world religions has ever questioned the truth that all our pain, including that which is directly caused by the operation of nature's laws, is a product of sin and ignorance. Nature holds the balance of good and evil, adjusting it continuously in accordance with God's providence and man's response; its alternations follow constantly the changing states of man. And this polarization of nature came about in that instant when I—when all mankind in me, and I in all mankind—preferred myself to God. That is what is being said in the story of Adam and Eve in the Garden of Paradise; and that is actually and factually the truth.

According to all the great traditions, while suffering is caused by evil, which is caused by sin, it has (given the fact of sin) a purpose, indeed a number of purposes. With varying degrees of emphasis, these may be listed as: retribution, restitution, learning and testing, sacrifice (which is at the same time a transformative operation and the restoration of a balance).

Retribution is simply the re-establishment of the state of justice. Justice is an attribute of God, which is held in a balance by mercy, but must always be fulfilled. This does not mean that we have the right, on our own personal responsibility, to punish each other. The administration of justice must always be conducted under God, under the auspices of the religious authority (in the Middle Ages it was frequently conducted actually within the walls of a church). As the state becomes more secularized, so-called "justice" becomes ever more unjustifiable, until civilized opinion veers towards sentimental leniency, which is the opposite of the spirit of revenge. Justice and mercy are one in God; and only as we exercise them faithfully under Him will they be one in us. God's justice punishes me for my sin. Whatever evil I must suffer is that punishment; and all the while God's mercy turns it to my greater good. By means of it I restore the balance that I, in my coinherence with the fallen Adam, as well as in my present life and former lives, have caused to tilt. Literally, I make amends; I mend the broken place. At the same time I learn to understand myself, to see what I have done. Slowly I begin to realize that the very fact of being born stamps me with an absolute responsibility for all the world's excruciating pain; since I myself am man, who turned his face away from God.

All this is implied in the Eastern concept of karma, which is perfectly consistent with the Christian doctrine of purgatory. These two apparently dissimilar teachings are alike in assuming that for each individual there exists a destiny extending through unimaginable eons of time, in the course of which every word, thought, and deed will receive its exact reward, and every wrong will be put right. In Christianity the predominant emphasis is upon the redemptive suffering to be found in the heart of sacrifice, the voluntary self-offering that leads through death to everlasting life. Prayers that, for centuries, have been repeated daily by Christians at the celebration of the Eucharist, if one reflects upon their meaning, are fraught with unthinkable terrors for all but the saints: "And here we offer and present unto thee, O Lord, ourselves, our souls and bodies, to be a reasonable, holy, and lively sacrifice . . ."

That is the prayer after Communion in the book of Common Prayer of the Church of England. The idea of sacrifice has to do with the restoration of a balance and it has to do with fire. Christ, in the final phase of his sacrificial action, ascends to heaven through the fire of the descending Spirit. (The Spirit descends three times in the myth, the Annunciation, the Baptism and Pentecost being three modes or aspects of a single event.) Every man, sooner or later, will pass through that fire. The idea of the "balance" is one of the more arcane themes of the ancient wisdom; it appears everywhere and is explained nowhere. Many lifetimes could be dedicated to its study; meanwhile, for beginners (by and for whom this book is being written), it is sufficient to understand that, since we have chosen to exist in a world of division, a world wherein the opposites have been turned one against the other (justice against mercy, order against freedom, and so on for every undivided attribute of the creator God), the balance of things is forever being tipped, and if it were not being continuously readjusted, the very substance of this world would fall apart. Existence depends upon a balance. This balance is preserved in the natural order by a ceaseless process of sacrifice in the form of assimilation and death. The realms of nature die into one another and are reborn. Rumi associates this process with the act of love:

Love is a boundless ocean, in which the heavens are
but a flake of foam.
Know that all the wheeling heavens are turned by waves
of Love: were it not for Love, the world would be
frozen.
How else would an inorganic thing change into a plant?
How would vegetative things sacrifice themselves to
become endowed with the animal spirit?
How would the animal spirit sacrifice itself for the sake
of that breath by the waft whereof a Mary was made
pregnant?. . .[1]

The Manichaean Gnostics said of Jesus that he hung
from every tree and was served up bound in every dish.
He is the "murdered, slaughtered soul" who rises, by
successive acts of self-sacrifice through all the levels of
creation. According to one description [from the *Kephalalaia
of Mani*] he passes through "the fruits, the cucumbers and
seed, which are beaten, plucked, torn to pieces, and give
nourishment to the worlds of flesh." The seemingly inborn
impulse of all men everywhere to offer sacrifices, often of
a bloody and horrible character, to the heavenly powers,
finds its consummation in the Christian teaching that Man-
in-God sacrifices Himself for the world in compensation
for the otherwise fatally downward-dragging effect of
human sin. This is the cosmic sacrifice. It is represented
as a crucifixion because the splaying out of the figure on
the Cross signifies that Christ's body is being pulled apart
in all the directions of space, and yet is able to remain intact
by virtue of the principle of Divinity within Himself. The
shedding of his blood from the five wounds representing
the senses nailing the soul to the world of space and time,
cries out for an end to bloodshed and makes possible the
bloodless sacrifice that is offered daily by the Church.

The ultimate sacrifice whereby man, in union with God, dies to his own nature, enabling that nature to arise in God and ascend to the heavenly state, has been defined, in the Christian religion, with a care that is no longer appreciated as having been essential to a right understanding of Christianity. The doctrines relating to the two natures of Christ, and the way in which the two natures are present in one man, are not only the very basis of Christian metaphysical thought; their implications extend into every sphere of human existence, adjusting the perspective whereby the individual views his world and society regulates its daily life. God does not suffer; man suffers. But man, insofar as he accepts the descent of God's mercy, is suffering in union with the Godhead within his own heart. In that union, by means of his suffering, he returns. Suffering is, in essence, the impact of evil. It is the tension produced by that impact, symbolized by the stretching outwards of the limbs and nerves of the victim impaled upon the Cross. As the evil passes into us and through us, we are faced with the alternatives of resisting it by anger, defending ourselves against it by selfishness, or accepting it as suffering, to be consumed in our sacrifice. The choice of this third alternative is what it means to be "in Christ."

Meister Eckhart declared: "In none of Christ's sufferings did his Godhead come to the help of his manhood." A terrible saying, but its meaning is that, as the same master writes elsewhere, "when the Son in his Godhead was pleased to be made man, and was, and suffered martyrdom, God's motionless detachment was no more disturbed than if he had never been made man." Jesus, in the sacred myth, is comforted and sustained by the ministry of angels, until the moment comes when the selfhood of his human nature must be sacrificed[2] so that only his God-nature remains. Yet, because of the union of the two natures, his human nature is sustained in the dimensionless point of its extinction (at the crossing of all the dimensions of space and time, where they are torn apart by sin). Meanwhile, throughout the enactment of the Mystery, the Godhead itself, being changeless and immovable in itself, remains immovable and unchanged. That is what Meister Eckhart, in conformity with the orthodoxy of the Church down through the ages, was attempting to explain. And do we imagine that this is some hair-splitting theological argument, with no reference to our everyday concerns? If so, we are mistaken. Traditional theology arose out of metaphysical knowledge. A lack of metaphysical knowledge is the root cause of all the problems that beset us, individually and in our social and political relationships.

All through recorded history, in every corner of the world, the Divine Victim dies and is reborn. In the Hindu cosmogony He is called Purusha (Man). The cosmos is made in the image of Purusha. Before this happened He was alone; then he was cut in pieces as a sacrifice, and out of the parts of his body were created all things that are in heaven and on earth. In Germanic mythology He is Ymir: "From the flesh of Ymir the world was formed, from his blood the billows of the sea, the hills from his bones . . ." and so on. The Christian Mystery of the Passion is fed by the same stream of primordial wisdom that flowed through the Orphic teachings, nourishing Plato and Plotinus. G. R. S. Mead, writing in the last decade of the nineteenth century, said: "The Eleusinian, Orphic, Bacchic, Samothracian, Phrygian, Egyptian, Chaldean, and other Mysteries all came from a common source." All have to do, fundamentally, with the meaning of death and rebirth, sacrifice, and the ambiguity of sexual love. The Christian Cross is a sexual symbol, as surely as the Hindu lingam, which represents the phallus of the god.

The Crucifixion is the supreme ritual of displacement. The law of the "balance" involves a perpetual exchange.

In the play of creation, light passes over into darkness, darkness into light, until the moment comes when the balance tips and the all-darkness becomes the all-light; whereupon there proceeds from it once more its eternal twin, and the cosmic process begins once again, the process of time, the process of return. Sacrifice effects displacement. Death pays for life; life necessitates death. Deep in this mystery lies the explanation of the extraordinary ambiguity of traditional attitudes towards sex. This ambiguity is universal. If it is most clearly evident in Christianity, the reason is that Christianity is supremely the religion to emphasize the suffering introduced into the world by sin, that is to say, by the soul's rejection of its necessary death in love. The process of dying into God, whereby creation returns and the many are reabsorbed into the One, becomes an anguish of crucifixion only when seen from the perspective of a world gone wrong. In such a world the returning turns against itself. An act of murderous rage replaces one of absolute surrender to the will of God. The orgasm of ecstasy becomes the cry of dereliction from the Cross; and all things are seen, for one appalling instant, in reverse. That is why the entire drama of the Passion can be shown to be, in every detail of its symbolism, a veiled and agonizing presentation of the sexual act.

The Cross itself is the dark aspect of the Bride of God. The nuptials of the Virgin in heaven represent her emergence from the powers of her own negativity: they take place on the other side of cosmic death. This symbolism is confirmed, in the Church's liturgical worship, by innumerable litanies, prayers, and hymns which extol the Cross in words very similar to those which are addressed to the Virgin Herself. Far from denouncing the instrument of Christ's Passion, Christians down the ages have prayed to it, kissing its relics with as much devotion as if they were Our Lady's hands and feet. In the Middle Ages no high altar could be dedicated until a relic of the "True Cross" had been placed beneath it. St. Anselm was being in no way eccentric when he prayed: "Dear Cross . . . precious wood . . . worshipful sign . . . By thee the world is made new and adorned with the light of truth . . . by thee the holy celestial city is rebuilt . . . In thee and by thee is my salvation and my life." And the great Good Friday hymn known as the *Pange Lingua*[3] has the antiphon repeated five times:

Crux fidelis inter omnes
Abor una nobilis:
Nulla silva talem profert
Fronde, flore, germine.

Faithful Cross, of trees created,
Noblest tree of all art thou.
Forest none bears trees as thou art,
Like in leaf or flower or bough.

Here we have a link with the Tree of Life, the Cosmic Axis linking the many levels of being, World Tree of a thousand names. An extraordinary painting by the fourteenth-century artist Simone dei Crociffissi depicts the Virgin asleep upon her bed, the World Tree sprouting like a phallus from her womb, bearing upon its branches the crucified figure of the Christ. The expression on her face is one of passive ecstasy. The laden Tree, in her dream, represents at the same time her own androgynous fulfillment and the heavenly Bridegroom in the act of love. "The Cross has become his marriage bed . . . his bitter death bears thee to sweet life" (Ephraem Syrus). One of the great holy days of the Church is the feast of the Exaltation of the Cross. This is described exoterically in terms of the rediscovery of the Cross by the Empress Helena, mother of Constantine; but its inner meaning is revealed in paintings of its assumption into heaven, borne upwards by angels in a manner corresponding to the Virgin's own ascent. For indeed the two are made one. The feast of the Coronation of the Virgin celebrates the consummation of God's union with man's soul, as spotless Virgin, bloodied Cross — and that other Mary, who represents the pilgrimage in time whereby the soul in bonds completes the circle of its earthly life.

For the Christian Church the act of sex within marriage is a sacrament. (It is not always realized that the act itself is the sacrament, the partners being regarded as assuming a role not unlike that of officiating priests.) Its prohibition in any other context arose from the idea that human sexuality is always either intentionally sacramental or a grievous sin, because it coinheres on the one hand with with the mystical union between Christ and the Virgin (God and man's soul), on the other with the Passion and the Death. Insofar as there is here a confusion of thought, it belongs to the exoteric interpretation of an esoteric truth. The sacramental life, or life "in Christ" is not to be confined within the forms devised for it by men, not even when those forms have been inspired by the Spirit within the context of a living faith. The very words "in Christ," appearing as they do to apply only to the Christian religion, are liable to mislead. Rumi (whose works must surely have been known to Shakespeare, that master of the ancient wisdom) wrote of the significance and insignificance of names and forms:

> Do you know any name without a reality?
> Or have you ever plucked a rose from R.O.S.E.?[4]
> You have pronounced the name: go, seek the thing named.

The "thing named" in this case is a sexual relationship in which the partners consciously submit themselves to the

action of a love that is higher than that of either the physical
or the psychical nature, and which, insofar as it is present,
implies fidelity, sharing, and regeneration; in practice, not
an easy path outside the context of a fully functioning
traditon to which both partners owe obedience.

In medieval churches it was customary to exhibit the
Rood on a beam above the sanctuary entrance. This group
consists of Our Lady and St. John standing on either side
of the crucified Christ. In the art of painting, this theme
is frequently extended to include the Magdalen, who kneels
with unbound hair at the foot of the Cross. The veiled
sun and moon may appear above the heads of the man
and the woman, who stand divided and facing one another
across the symbol of sexual opposition and of death. The
Virgin and St. John are the two figures in the myth who,
for different reasons, are immune from the sufferings
brought about by sin. The Virgin is adored under three
aspects by the Church: as Joyful, Sorrowful, and Glorious.
Her Sorrowful Mysteries are associated with the Passion,
and with those events in the story that foreshadow the
Passion. In her sorrowful aspect she weeps. A much valued
devotion represents her with seven swords piercing the
spiritual heart at the midpoint of the breast. In the Pieta
scene she is holding the limp body of the Crucified in her
arms, mother and lover, mourning over the Beloved. There
remains, however, a sharp distinction between her *sorrow*
and the *sufferings* of the Christ. Her body suffers no outrage
or disfigurement; "There shall no defiled thing fall into her."
She is perfect purity, in which nothing that is impure,
nothing that is not of God, can linger for an instant. The
world cannot touch her. Her Son descends into the depths
of matter, is crushed by its density, wounded, humiliated,
besmirched, subjected to the final ignominy of death. The
Virgin remains beautiful to the end (in Michaelangelo's
mystical Pieta she is still in her first youth) and does not

die but falls asleep. The significance here is that she represents the opposite choice from that which brought into existence death and pain. Between two polarized alternatives every man must choose; and in the choice the Blessed Virgin makes in us we all are saved in Christ. She, in her own person, is the unfallen center of the human soul, perceived by Julian as a "full fair creature"; in most of us still but a "little child," albeit grown to maturity in the saints. The Church, in its cult of Mary, has taught its children to cling to that which, in themselves, is the mediating principle between the soul and God. It is not that we should reduce the figure of the Blessed Virgin to some abstract notion that has no personification in the heavenly state, but that we should adore in her, as wholly real and substantial in herself, the soul of man adorned with beauty as the One Beloved. The cult of the Virgin Mary is no consolatory indulgence; neither is it a metaphysical game. As food is to the body, so is the prayer of attention to the archetype of absolute purity essential to the growth in spirituality of the soul.

St. John the Beloved Disciple is exempt from the pains and disfigurements represented by the Cross for another reason. "Son, behold thy Mother"; these words of the dying Christ foretell the role St. John is to play in the next cycle of creation. This destiny implies that the one who must endure it has reached the end of his pilgrimage in time. It is here that we find the teachings of Christianity and of Buddhism approaching one another in a manner which is all the more striking because the modes of expression are so different. The Bodhisattva is one who, having achieved the goal of readiness to enter Nirvana, chooses not to do so until all beings are able to enter with him "down to the smallest blade of grass." In a state of serene detachment he remains in time while time remains. In a future cycle he becomes the Buddha, after which he will pass away and another—his beloved disciple—will take his place. Similarly, the second St. John has passed beyond the need to work out his salvation in the bonds of time. Now there is nothing left to do but choose, at the foot of the cross, to become himself the future Christ.

St. John, we are told, did not suffer martyrdom as did the other apostles. Attempts by his enemies to destroy him were miraculously frustrated, and so he lived on to the age of ninety-nine before disappearing from the sight of men. (It is interesting that both St. John and Ananda, the Buddha's beloved disciple, are the subject of legends to the effect that they have not died but are "in hiding," either in the sense of having become invisible, or in that of being hidden in a cave until the world's end. Christ Himself, in his words to Peter, implied that John would "tarry till I come." And it is John who is, traditionally, the author of the book of Revelation, which describes how he was taken out of time to behold the Day of Judgment.) A particularly beautiful legend relates how, on reaching this age, he gathered his disciples about him, repeating again and again, "My children, love one another." Then he caused a grave to be dug beneath the altar of his church, and descended into it, praying, there to be enveloped like the phoenix in a blinding light and fire, in the midst of which he vanished. (The phoenix, which expires in flames and is reborn, has been regarded both as a type of Christ and as a symbol of St. John.) Afterwards the grave was found to be filled with manna which gave forth a heavenly fragrance. Manna is the "bread from heaven," type of the Body of Christ. This, then, was all that was left of the transmuted body of the Beloved.[5]

The first St. John, as the Christ Child's human nature or human "twin," is an even more mysterious figure, representing, in some way that cannot be logically "explained," the previous St. John, who now appears in the role of Christ. We may see him as the human "garment" put aside and left behind as its wearer travelled on. In his martyrdom, he represents the human interface between Christ's God-united human nature and the lower realms, which, passing upwards through Him, are offered in an outpouring of human blood from the artery which drains the heart. The symbolism of the severed head is connected with fertility rites and with the sun. It typifies both the instinctive sacrifices whereby primitive societies sought to propitiate their gods, and the ultimate oblation of nature in its role of making possible the Holy Birth. If the Word is to become flesh in a divine descent, there must be, at the same time, an ascent of the natural soul, which will pour itself out in the making of the Body of the Lord. The superior vitality of the child St. John will pass to his "cousin" in the rite of sacrifice by Herod's knife. "He must increase; I must decrease." These words will no longer baffle us when we read them in the context of that mythological event.

It must be stressed, in case the point has even now been insufficiently clarified, that a mythological event of the order of significance under discussion is not to be regarded as something that "never happened." The events of a sacred myth are infinitely more real than any we are likely to recapture if our science leads us to a method of bringing back the historic past, our own particular "line of time," as a "video" on our television sets. By that means the most we should see would be an illusion. It is impossible to say how Jesus would appear to us within the context of that illusion, because one cannot deduce from the gospels the extent to which they are based upon "history" as distinct from myth.

The metaphysics of sacrifice constitute, for most of us at least, a depth of knowledge that will remain unfathomable until the end of time. But we can gaze into those depths and be refreshed, and understand our own lives the better in consequence. Meditation on such Mysteries as that of the two St. Johns may seem to be leading us into strange byways, but it is not an impractical exercise. A living idea will create a ferment in the mind, and can bring about permanent changes in the mental and spiritual states of the one who assimilates that idea by means of the symbology appropriate to it. From an immediately practical point of view, if certain key ideas are no longer implicit in the very structure of the way we live, as a result of being condensed and symbolized in the structure of our worship, it becomes necessary for us somehow to rediscover those ideas, before we can make even the smallest decisions in relation to our day-to-day concerns. For our day-to-day concerns are based upon metaphysical truth.

11

What Is, What Was,
What Will Be?

Only in the context of his life in eternity can we understand man's life in time. This is not, however, a question of what is sometimes called the "afterlife." Eternity is present in time; time is suffused with eternity; the one cannot be understood without the other. What does have to be realized is that what we think of as a "lifetime" is an infinitesimally tiny fragment of the total destiny in time of the individual who is passing through it. Not to see that is to ascribe to transitory circumstances an importance that is out of all proportion to their true significance.

Circumstances are the exteriorization of states. Time itself is no more than the passage of the soul from one state to another, in accordance with its own choices and its own deeds. Our world, as we experience it, is the intersection of all possible states (so when we see pictures or read descriptions of heaven and hell, these are but ways of depicting the twin poles of our own world, our own experience, our own states, between which there is purgatory and paradise and that strange land of dreams that

Islam calls the realm of the djinn—and everything else that the human heart contains within itself). The circumstances that overtake me today may be the the outcome of something which seemed, when it happened, to be a very small thing, scarcely noticed by anyone else, a choice maybe that I made as a tiny child in the faroff past of the world, and am in danger of making again in some age that is to come. Such a choice is significant "for a time"; its repercussions must work themselves out; but the circumstances it produces for me are no more in themselves than my perception of the world as the world has been modified by my choice: agonizing as the circumstances may very well be, they can last no longer than the state I have chosen to inhabit.

For we do actually inhabit our own states. If we were not doing that we should inhabit God's; we should be in heaven, because after all, there is only heaven. Our states, in the bondage of time, are illusions that we bring upon ourselves. They emerge from our wrong choices, which themselves emerge from that first wrong choice that we call "original sin," made in the instant when time as we know it was set upon its spiralling course. Time *as we know it*. . . But there are other ways of knowing time. Plato describes time as "the moving image of eternity." Angelus Silesius reminds us:

> Eternity is as time, time is as eternity,
> If they are otherwise, the difference is in thee.

So we must assume that there is, in God, a divine mode of time, which is "as eternity," the movement of Love within itself. Time as we know it is very different. In the East it is seen as a relentless wheel of recurring births and deaths from which all creatures aspire to escape. (It is marvelously ironic that Westerners should turn to the oriental religions to satisfy the sort of avid interest in "reincarnation" that no oriental religion would encourage for a moment.) This image of the wheel appears in Christianity as the symbol associated with St. Catherine of Alexandria, who appears in sacred art in the act of receiving a bridal ring from the infant Christ. St. Catherine is said to have been martyred on a wheel, for which reason she has become a type of the human soul who, having been martyred on the wheel of time, receives the ring of eternity as her reward.[1]

Modern physics presents us with the idea of space-time as an indivisible continuum, of time as having no objective existence in itself. This negation of our habit-formed notions of time can be deeply alarming unless we are able to see time in its positive as well as in its negative aspect, as leading us into eternity, its spiralling turned in the direction from which we came and by which we must now return. Seen in this perspective, space-time is the winding and unwinding of eternity. Silesius again says:

> Man should essential be;
> For when this world is gone
> All accident is past,
> The essence still lives on.

If we trust time because it, too, is a creature of God, it will carry us to our goal. Time is an aspect of Maya; it can conceal and mislead, but it can also make manifest. It is relative in the sense of being subjective-objective, like every other phenomenon of human existence. Each one of us knows for himself the mystery that lies hidden in the vast differences of speed-in-time that we secretly experience. The time of a small child, compared with that of an adult, passes so slowly that its days are as wonder-filled years, its years as a decade will seem later on.[2] When we tread a tiny insect thoughtlessly underfoot, we do not consider that the time of its pain may be unimaginably longer in its experience than in our own. A forest has its own time, which is not the same as that of one of its trees. I *am* my own time. As we begin to understand how this can be, we begin to be ready to think about what is so misleadingly described as the "afterlife."

Nietzche wrote, "This life is my eternal life." Could he have meant by this that a single life from birth to death was all the time allotted to his pilgrim soul? Surely not, for he says "my *eternal* life." The violent paradox, the lack of ordinary human logic, is apparent. Nietzche had insights about time that eventually drove him mad; or was it the "madness" in his soul that enabled him to see visions closed to the vast majority of his fellow human beings, of time forever spiralling in infinity and returning upon itself? It would seem that he had come into contact with a certain ancient teaching which resolves the paradox of his otherwise inexplicable statement by suggesting that a single life may indeed revolve eternally in a state of perpetual change. The soul has the task of returning this life to its source, and does so in a time that continually recurs until its process is complete. The moment of conception is one with the moment of death; and so, in death, the soul can pass through eternity back to the beginning of the circle of the life that has come to an end. It is not, as we are tempted to imagine, a question of "again and again"; but of working on the life as a whole, in such a way that a single directional change, brought about by submission of the will, from the center of the self, will alter not only the future but the past. The whole life, in a higher dimension, is a body that can grow and change, becoming more spiritualized or more degenerate. Important relationships will change, because the same people will be encountered at different stages of their own journeyings in time, according to the responses one is willing to make, the debts one is willing to pay, the extent to which one is willing to be forgiven and to forgive.[3]

"Reincarnation" is another subject. In the swirling pathways of all times there is room for as many lives for each one of us as there are stars in the firmament. But still, at the end of my journeyings all my times will be gathered into one; and after all there will have been, for me, one single ever-changing time that has been, all the time, my "eternal life." Meanwhile, it is surely less profitable to dwell upon imaginative reconstructions of one's adventures in ancient Egypt than it is to discover how one's present tiny span, no moment of which shall ever pass away, may be redeemed and given back to God. "That which hath been is now; and that which is to be hath already been; and God requireth that which is past" (Ecclesiastes 3:15).

12

What Is Meant by the "Afterlife"?

Christianity speaks of three states associated with the "life after death." These three are purgatory, heaven, and hell. In reality, all three should be seen as intersecting this world and this life. We experience at least two of them *here* and *now*. (Eternal hell is the state where God is not. The possibility of this being actually experienced by any human soul is not one that can or should be contemplated further than to admit that it exists.) The significance of their being situated in the "afterlife" is that the moment of death is imagined as being the one in which we recognize and are assigned to the state to which, at that moment, we belong. Heaven is the state of being with God, from which, save in the capacity of a world-savior, there is no obligation to return. Purgatory is the negative aspect of time, in which the soul is self-imprisoned until, of its own free will, it releases itself. Therefore, purgatory represents a return from the timeless moment of death into the bonds of time until one's time has been worked out.

The Roman Catholic Church has emphasized the association of purgatory with time in some rather curious ways. Little cards instructing the faithful that the repetition of a certain prayer so many times would remit so many years of the purgatory earned by one's sins became, and remained for many years, a prominent part of the everyday paraphernalia of Catholic churches all over the world. (It was not always remembered that the purity of one's state of mind was an absolute condition for the efficacy of this arrangement!) A kind of supernatural commerce was introduced, whereby "merits" could be exchanged, these being a sort of coinage representing the remission of purgatorial "time," which could be requested from the saints (who, by definition, had more than they any longer needed to use) or generously offered from one's own meager store on behalf of someone else. Small wonder if these practices disappeared in the aftermath of Vatican II. And yet their disappearance has been tragic, insofar as the great metaphysical truths that had hitherto been preserved, albeit in atrophied forms, instead of being released from these forms, have been rejected with them.

Mandean gnosticism presents us with fearful images of the soul wandering, like the Magdalen, in the interstices of time:

> Having once strayed into the labyrinth of evils
> the wretched one finds no way out. . .
> She seeks to escape from the bitter chaos
> and knows not how she shall get through.
> Naasene Psalm

This idea of time as bondage is common to all the traditions. It is purgatory, it is the wandering of the Magdalen in the streets and byways of the city, it is the wheel, the labyrinth, the swaddling bands that spiral tightly round the helpless body of the newborn Christ. Always it has to be seen as a state—the state of being imprisoned and lost—never as a definition of "this world," which presents the possibility of all possible states because it is their meeting point. Purgatory, at its worst, is a state of frightful pain. But those who are undergoing it are called by the Church the "holy souls" because to be in this state implies that one has made the choice to be with God. The "holy souls," having made their choice, have not yet been purged of all that holds them back. Now they are being tenderly prepared for their encounter with the fire of God's love. If the preparation is by pain—how else?

The saints are, by definition, those who have freed themselves—or rather, willed themselves to be freed—from the bonds of time. They have entered heaven. Here again, by the time the reaction set in, the legalistic tendencies of the Vatican had been running amok for so long that the canonization of a saint was more like a vastly expensive and unbelievably complicated proceeding in the law courts than what it was actually supposed to be—a conference of the hierarchy for the purpose of meditating upon holiness and bearing witness to it. The result of all this fearful cranking of ecclesiastical machinery was presented as a cast-iron guarantee to the faithful that the new saint could be prayed *to* (instead of *for*, as was appropriate in the case of a "holy soul") and was qualified to produce miracles and merits in response. A novena (nine days of prayer) was, for some reason unexplained (because long forgotten by all concerned), prescribed as being peculiarly efficacious in moving even the most hard-of-hearing of the saints. So were the faithful instructed in what it means to be, at last, with God; and the formulas, for all their cumbersomeness and rigidity, were metaphysically accurate. The saints are in God's presence; and we, poor "holy souls," must cling to the hem of their garments ("clinging heaven by the hems,"

as Francis Thompson wrote), praying to be raised up into
their Sabbath peace. The Sabbath Day represents the
gathering up into eternity of all the strands of time. Six
is the number of time: six days of creation, six ages of the
world, six ages of man, six waterpots to be filled with the
waters of the river of life to be changed into the wine of
eternity by the presence of Christ. Seven is the number
of rest. The Sabbath of a saint is the day of his death, which
is celebrated thereafter as his feast.

The word *hell*, wherever it occurs, should be treated
warily because it means different things in different contexts.
In the Creed it refers to limbo, the nadir of density from
which it is possible to escape by the light of Christ, as we
see in the story of his "descent into hell" to rescue the
trapped souls. This is an aspect of purgatory: the timeless
instant, on the turn of the spiral, of darkness and impotence
"before" the return journey is able to begin. The more usual
meaning of *hell* is the everlasting fire of the Divine Being,
which is known as unimaginable anguish by the one who
refuses to repent. This dreadful image is accompanied by
a stern prohibition against assuming that anyone is, or ever
will be, self-consigned to such a fate. The state of hell is
affirmed as a possibility (and therefore as existent) in view
of the absolute freedom of the human will, and the
undeniable power of the twisted will to sever God's wrath
from His mercy in the human heart. Yet Julian of Norwich
was convinced that such a severance will not be permitted
to exist beyond the end of time. "There is a Deed," she
says, "the which the blessed Trinity shall do in the Last
Day, as to my sight, and when the Deed shall be, and how
it shall be done, is unknown of all creatures that are beneath
Christ, and shall be till when it is done . . . This is that
Great Deed ordained of our Lord God from without
beginning, treasured and hid in His blessed breast, only
known to Himself: by which He shall make all things well."

We cannot imagine, any more than Julian could, how this is to be brought about. We only know, as she did, that on the Last Day of the present great cycle of time, the totality of darkness will be returned and become the totality of light.

Meanwhile, there is God's promise that the tiniest motion of repentance will call down his mercy and turn the soul towards heaven. Islam has the following tradition, cited by Rumi's translator, R. A. Nicholson:

> When God has finished judging mankind on the day of Resurrection, two men will remain and the order will be given that both are for Hell. Then on the way thither one of them will turn his face to God, and the Almighty will order him to be brought back and will ask him why he turned round, and he will answer, "I was hoping Thou wouldst let me enter Paradise." And then God will order that he be taken to Paradise.

One is reminded of the Dying Thief.

The Church teaches that each soul, in the moment of death, undergoes a "particular" judgment. This is distinguished from the universal judgment of the Last Day; and there would appear to be a discrepancy until one recalls that, in eternity, "times" have no absolute length, and intersect at the point where their circles are complete. Judgment is irreversible in all the traditions. The soul is sealed as belonging irrevocably to its final state. (This is the judgment called "of the Last Day," although, since it takes place in eternity, we participate in it already in this life.) The "particular" judgment represents the assignment of a "time," which must pass before the final judgment is effectually carried out. This is the meaning of purgatory, as has previously been explained. The soul, having arrived in death at the end of time, receives both the irreversible judgment relating to its final state, and the "particular"

judgment whereby it is sent back for a given time to work
out its salvation in suffering and "good works."

An obvious, and hence ubiquitous, image for the
"particular" judgment is the weighing of the soul, by an
angelical being, in a pair of scales. This scene is represented
in the iconography of ancient Egypt, in Zoroastrianism,
Christianity, and the Buddhism of Tibet. Here again is the
concept of a balance. If the soul sinks beneath the weight
of its evil deeds, a balance is upset and must be readjusted
by means of "purgatory" or "karma." (The reality is the same,
although the names and the imagery are different.)
Judgment, however, can be unexpected; for God's thoughts
about us are not our thoughts. Many old games have their
origin in metaphysics. The children's game of "Snakes and
Ladders" is a salutory reminder of a teaching common to
all the traditions with regard to the "particular" judgment.
The seemingly dedicated and enlightened man who comes
to die with a spark of pride in his heart will be like the
apparently winning player in the game, who makes a final
throw for the goal and finds himself sliding back to his
starting point down the tail of the "Great Snake."
Conversely, the "Great Ladder," which carries the losing
player right up the board to "heaven," may be seen as a
single act of disinterested love, one cry to be forgiven, which
bypasses in an instant a lifetime's failures, weaknesses, and
sins. Included in the "traditions" of Muhammad is the
following saying, put into the mouth of God:

> So long as you call upon Me and hope in Me,
> I forgive you all that originates from you: and I will
> not heed, O son of man,
> should your sins reach the horizon of the heavens, and
> then you asked my pardon,
> and I would pardon you.

And a Sufi hymn known as the Birth Song of the Prophet contains these lines:

Who says: Allah! in language truly loving
shall see his sins, like autumn leaves removing.

13

How Shall I Learn To Die?

We hear a great deal these days about the medical definition of death, and about a number of, in many cases beautiful and moving, psychical experiences of the process of dying, after the individual has lost consciousness and seems to be separating from the physical body. These accounts are related by persons who have been resuscitated after a near-death experience. Because in some cases the heart had temporarily stopped beating, they are quoted as if they were descriptions of death itself. But death, in the religious traditions, is defined as the moment from which there is no coming back. It is essentially a spiritual rather than a psychical experience. It takes us momentarily out of time.

The Tibetan *Bardo Thodol,* which is a scripture entirely devoted to the soul's existence between death and rebirth, starts with a description of how, in the moment of death, the soul, for an instant in-and-out of time, comes face to face with Truth. This encounter is called in the *Bardo* "the perceiving of the Clear Light." The Light, unveiled and unalloyed, is unbearable to the unpurified soul. Only by recognizing and enduring it can one hope to achieve union with it and be released from the necessity of return to the wheel of birth and death. But who is capable of doing this? So the dying person is exhorted: "O nobly born, listen. Now thou art experiencing the Radiance of the Clear Light of Pure Reality. Recognize it . . . keep thyself in the state of the divine mind of the Buddha."

In the vast majority of cases, however, the soul, being as yet unfit to remain in this state, passes on—precisely as, in the Christian version of the same experience, all but the saints enter purgatory, not primarily to receive punishment, but because they are themselves unwilling, and therefore unable, to endure God's presence. In the *Bardo,* the soul then sinks through a succession of states, and returns to a human birth. The point being made in this scripture is the need for the dying person to be aware of the experience of death and how to meet that experience. All the traditions emphasize this point. In the Middle Ages there was a considerable body of writings known collectively as the *Ars Moriendi,* the *Art of Dying.* A typical instruction is as follows:

> If you would learn good and evil go from home, go out of yourself, that is go out of this world and learn to die; send your soul from your body by thinking; send your heart into that other world; into heaven or hell or purgatory, and there you shall see what is good and what is evil. For in hell you shall see more sorrow than any man can describe, and in purgatory more torments than any man could endure, in Paradise more joy than any man could desire.

Of primary importance is the art of dying in this life. "Die before thou diest, so as not to die when thou diest." In the testimonies of the mystics of every faith, this advice of Angelus Silesius recurs more times than one can count, frequently in almost the same words. The meaning is twofold: that one should will to make the total sacrifice of the lower self before this is demanded inexorably by death, and that one should strive to imagine one's own death. For this exercise various pictorial images have been prescribed (the experience itself being presumed to be in the form of images chosen either deliberately or unconsciously by the subject). One such image, which appears in a number of traditions, including Christianity, is that of death as a bridge. "Brig o' Dread" is the name given to this bridge in the old north country song-poem for the eve of All Saints (Hallowe'en), which is the commemoration of All Souls. The Zoroastrian canon [*Avesta*] contains the following description: "For three days and nights the soul sits beside the pillow of the body. And on the fourth day at dawn the soul will reach the lofty and awful Cinvat Bridge to which every man must come."

On the near side of this bridge stands a being of light, a maiden named Daena, of whom the prepared and purified soul will inquire: "who art thou, whose beauty outshines all other beauty ever contemplated in the terrestrial world?" Then she, who is his heavenly counterpart, his perfected self, will embrace him and conduct him instantly to heaven. The awful bridge need never again be traversed; time, for this soul, is at an end. Clearly this is simply another way of describing the experience of the Clear Light. For those who have still to work out their time,[1] being as yet unfit to behold the celestial vision, the maiden appears either heavily veiled or, in the case of a hardened sinner, disguised as a frightful hag, his own negativity which he refuses to relinquish.

These are awesome images. Tradition has never flinched from depicting the soul's passing as a terrifying experience for all who do not come to it in a state of simplicity and self-abandonment. To refuse this understanding is untraditional and false. Yet in our own day the two great Churches of Rome and Canterbury, as part of the general mutilation of their marvelous liturgies, have removed from their burial services and prayers for the dying the least suggestion of fearfulness. Until recently it was accepted without question that the Church did not celebrate the deaths of the faithful, but reserved its rejoicings over death for the feast days of its canonized saints. The beautiful and awe-inspiring hymn known as the *Dies irae* used to be said or sung at every requiem mass in a Catholic church, all eighteen verses of it, without a light breaking through until the end, a cry torn from the heart of the dying in their consciousness of having so often turned from God. The end is hope; but hope in the infinite mercy of Christ towards the sinner whose only merit is repentance:

> *Pie Jesu Domine,*
> *Dona eis requiem. Amen.*

In the Church of England Prayer Book the words appointed to be said as the coffin is lowered into the grave are:

> Man that is born of a woman hath but a short time to live and is full of misery. He cometh up, and is cut down like a flower; he fleeth as it were a shadow, and never continueth in one stay. In the midst of life we are in death. Of whom may we seek for succor, but of thee O Lord, who for our sins art justly displeased? Yet O God most holy, O Lord most mighty, O holy and merciful Saviour, thou most worthy Judge eternal, suffer us not at our last hour for any pains of death to fall from thee.

And, as the first sprinkling of earth is cast upon the coffin, the great paradox is solemnly proclaimed:

. . . earth to earth, ashes to ashes, dust to dust, in sure
and certain hope of the Resurrection to eternal life.

Unreality comforts no one. In our hearts we understand
the truth of our self-imposed exile from God, and all the
sorrow and misery that is continuously being brought upon
us by our sin. To remove all reminders of what we know,
to pretend that we do not know it, is a pointless exercise.
In the same way, it is useless to pretend that the fearful
descriptions of the Last Day, the Day of Judgment, to be
found in the scriptures of all the world religions can be
put aside as "irrelevant" to our preoccupations in the present.
The Last Day of the Great Cycle of Time is described as
being a thousand times more awful than our worst
imaginings of a nuclear holocaust. The very stars fall out
of the sky. God's wrath—which is the Divine Principle
concealed within and concealing his mercy, brought into
manifestation by our determination to divide the two
principles in ourselves and relate ourselves to the one by
rejecting the other—will destroy the worlds in a flame of
fire more searing by far than that of a thousand suns, saving
only those who have turned, at the last, in simple faith
to Him. For this is the end of our time. For each and every
being the allotted span of his pilgrimage has been traversed,
and all ends meet in God.

And I saw a new heaven and a new earth. For the first
heaven and the first earth were passed away; and there
was no more sea. And I John saw the holy city, new
Jerusalem, coming down from heaven, prepared as a
bride adorned for her husband. And I heard a great voice
out of heaven saying, "Behold the tabernacle of God
is with men, and he will dwell with them, and they
shall be his people, and God himself shall be with them,
and be their God. And God shall wipe away all tears
from their eyes; and there shall be no more death,

neither sorrow, nor crying, neither shall there be any
more pain: for the former things are passed away."

This vision of St. John, described in the book of
Revelation, at the conclusion of the Christian canon,
expands into ever more and more beautiful images:

And there shall be no night there; and they need no
candle, neither light of the sun; for the Lord giveth them
light: and they shall reign forever and ever.

The paradox is beyond our understanding. On the one
hand it is implicit in the Christian Mystery, as it is explicit
in Hinduism, that the great cycles of time will, like all the
lesser ones that turn within them, continue to revolve
"forever and ever" without end; on the other we are told
explicitly by St. John that all things come to their eternal
rest in God. How can we come to see that both these "ways
of putting it" are true?

And therefore when the Doom is given and we be all
brought up above, then shall we clearly see in God the
secret things which be now hid to us. Then shall none
of us be stirred to say in any wise: Lord, if it had been
thus, then it had been full well; but we shall say all with
one voice: Lord, blessed mayst thou be, for it is thus:
it is well; and now see we verily that all-thing is done
as it was then ordained before that anything was made.
                    Julian of Norwich

14

What Does It Mean To Be "In Christ"?

It is said that three things were forbidden to man before he conceived the sin of Adam in his heart; and that it was in prematurely claiming those three things that he committed sin. Not that God would not have bestowed them upon him in his own good time, for God created man with the purpose of making him his son; but the gifts of the Spirit are not to be appropriated as a right. They are intended to be held, under the limitations of obedience, in trust. Those three things were knowledge, ecstasy, and power.

Knowledge, ecstasy, and power were the God-given attributes of the Archangel Lucifer (who became Satan) that brought about his undoing when he flaunted them before God as if, on account of them, he were equal with God. Lucifer is man's angelical nature, as Adam is the bright, perfected flower of human nature in its primal innocence, before the angelical nature descends upon it. The Luciferian attributes were destined to be incorporated into man as man was raised above the state belonging to the paradisal garden to that of sonship in God's presence. Here, as so frequently happens, we encounter a difficulty in reconciling the meaning of the myth with the time-sequence of its events. As Adam, man is "not yet" in possession of his angelical nature, and yet it is that same angelical nature which causes him to sin. If the myth were to be read as an allegory, there would be no solution to this problem; because an allegory not only presents a logical sequence of episodes in time, it represents another, equally logical sequence of ideas that correspond exactly to its time-unfoldment. A myth, on the other hand, is a highly complex and subtle transposition into a sequential "story" of the various aspects of a single metaphysical event. Thus the fallen Lucifer (become Satan) in the garden who tempts Adamic man to disobedience is a part of the original wholeness of man himself. As we see in the Islamic version of the archangelical fall, the Lucifer-in-man refuses to bow down before the image of God that is represented by the human form. He rejects all earthly limitation. "Shall I bow down before a thing of clay?". . . .

The two myths of Lucifer complement one another. It is man's higher nature, that part of him that is more than merely human, more than the Adam (because it has been bestowed upon the Adam by the breath of God) that is the source of all his pride, and has caused him to refuse the formal limitations of his earthly state. In the same eternal instant as he receives the gift, he sins. He demands as his by right, those things that are now to be given him in trust to be enjoyed and used "in Christ." It is required of him to submit himself to the Christ Principle within the heart, whereby the fire of the Spirit will consume the lower self. And that, inflated by the taste of power, he will not do. So those things which he has demanded are forbidden him until he "turns again," and on a new way, in a new time, this time through the principle of opposition he himself has introduced, is reunited to the Christ within.

Knowledge, ecstasy, and power, because they are not ours by right, will be fatal to us, individually and collectively, save insofar as we are in that state which enables us to use them as they should be used. The Church has defined that state as being "in Christ." So what precisely does this mean? For until we can answer this question — until, that is to say, we know the answer in our hearts, whether we are capable of verbalizing it or not — we should not rightly dare to read a book or beget a child or switch on the electric light.

St. Paul wrote to the Corinthians, "If any man be in Christ he is a new creature: old things are passed away: behold all things are become new." These words employ the Christian formula to describe a state of being that may be described in as many other ways as there are holy traditions to provide those ways. The formula contains the reality, but it does not constrain the reality. Bearing this ever in mind, we shall stay with St. Paul, who is actually in the process of renewing and bringing together a number of strands from the ancient traditions and, subject to the guidance of the Holy Spirit, making something new; namely, the Christian faith. The words we have quoted are a description of the birth of God in the soul and of the soul in God. The letters of St. Paul take this Mystery as their predominant theme. The Christians to whom he wrote had been taught that when a man passes through the waters of baptism from the life of nature to the life of grace, he undergoes so complete a change that even the smallest and most trivial of his actions acquires a new significance. It is performed by the power of the Spirit, and is no longer his but Christ's.

Not surprisingly, in view of this belief, it was at first supposed that the rite of baptism conferred a state of grace in the sense that, being a "new man," the baptized person would never again be guilty of a grievous sin. When this was found to be an overly optimistic view of the situation, the sacrament of Penance was introduced as a means of restoring the penitent to his previous state. But the real problem went deeper than this. A mistaken view of the rite as having in itself an automatic effect, and of the visible institutional Church as being the sole vehicle upon earth of the reality it symbolically represents, was leading Christianity astray—not into heresy in the sense of a radical distortion of the faith, but into an exoteric misinterpretation of the truth. In the past, far more than at the present time (when we tend to fall into the opposite error, and blur the incisive outlines of a particualr formulation of the primary revelation), it was difficult for even the finest minds to avoid this kind of mistake.

On the exoteric level it is actually not possible to hold the paradox of a total identification of symbol with reality together with the understanding that no symbol is automatically efficacious of itself, and no symbol is the exclusive bearer of its own significance. It is, therefore, essential to the health of a tradition that the line of those who guide its historical course retains the knowledge of its esotericism (that is to say, of those teachings which can only be understood by the few whose spiritual eyesight has been developed beyond a certain point) and be able to hold the balance between that knowledge and the more simplistic interpretations that inevitably make their appearance. It is probable that there were, for a time at least, those within the Church who knew the "secret"—for such it was, in the sense that it would have been unwise to communicate it to an inexperienced neophyte, who would merely have been flung from one side of the paradox to the other with disastrous results[1]—of the transcendental unity of religions. Whether St. Paul was one of these it is hard to say, given the obvious limitations of existing evidence. By the end of the third century A.D., Christianity had taken on the character of a profoundly metaphysical Mystery religion having strong affinities with Orphism and the Egyptian tradition. The schools of mystical theology in Alexandria were creating a spiritual and intellectual ferment, in which the Christian faith was being molded in ways that have since been forgotten, although the results were to be ineradicable. However, the concept of the Church as containing an esoteric school at the heart of its priesthood was not to survive the enormous temptations of power represented by the mass conversions which made Christianity, under Constantine, the official religion of the West.

Meanwhile, the contradiction between what were assumed to be the automatic effects of baptism and the sad actuality, because this constituted a problem that was fully resolvable only at the highest level of understanding, became ever more painful and insistent. Within the religious Orders, an attempt was made to set apart a minority who vowed themselves to live by the example of the saints (the early Church had seen itself as a community of saints). But even in these self-protected enclaves the difficulties remained basically the same. They were partially, but not altogether, resolved in a growing understanding of the Christian life as a consciously chosen and divinely ratified direction in time. Where it had seemed at first that baptism represented time's fulfillment, after which there could be no true "after" but only a waiting for Christ's Second Coming, which was confidently expected to take place within the lifetime of the first Christians, it began to be realized that the world was going on, and that it was going on in very much the same manner as before. Baptism, for the vast majority of the faithful, did not bring about instantaneous sanctity, but sealed an intention, and opened up a means of fulfilling that intention in the course of time. So a new understanding was reached, whereby it was made explicit that a soul may be effectually reconciled with God by virtue of the direction in which the will is set (and here again we see why the expression "holy souls" was applied to those who, without having yet achieved their release from the time-bound state, had made their choice and so, in the mind of God, were numbered with the saints).

But how, it will be asked, if the will is free, can its final intention thus be sealed and known? The answer is that our choice is known in eternity because we choose, have chosen, and will choose in eternity; even while we work out our choice in this world, which is the intersection point of eternity with time and space. Purgatory is a concept that has been abstracted from "this world"; it represents the negative time-flow that impedes the aspiration of the soul, while purging it of those very impurities that are the cause of its being held back. The soul whose essentiality is orientated towards heaven is *moving out* of purgatory *into* the eternity in which its choice awaits it when its journey is complete. That is what Simone Weil (who exemplified, if anyone ever did, the true mystic who is not bound to any established faith) meant when she wrote: "The looking is what saves us." She advocated the setting up of "reminders" of the presence of Christ in every public place. "It should also be publicly and officially recognized that religion is nothing else but a looking." If this sounds a little strange, it will cease to do so when we realize that she is here equating the act of "looking" with that of "turning towards" or intentionally orientating oneself.

In many traditions enormous importance is attached to the circumnambulation of a sacred place in the direction taken by the sun. This is a formal recognition of the truth that everything depends upon the direction in which we are choosing to move along the time-spiral that can lead us towards or away from our goal. According to the law

of correspondences, whereby the forms of the natural world
correspond to the unseen realities of the metaphysical
realms, the sunwise direction here on earth corresponds
to that of the soul's return to its origin in God. The negative
time-flow runs counter to that direction; in meeting it we
encounter "purgatory" or "suffering" (that is to say, we
encounter *evil,* which is turned to our good insofar as we
experience it as suffering instead of converting it to sin).
To walk in the way of the sun is to be "in Christ." It is
that state in which we are permitted, within the Order of
the World,[2] and where possible, within the context of a
living and operative religion to which we owe obedience,
to receive in a new mode, not as contaminated powers but
as a pure influx from the realms above, those spiritual gifts
which pertain to the angelical nature of the sons of God.

Knowledge, ecstasy, and power . . . how soon, if ever,
shall we, as a collectivity, we, the human race, perceive
what the claiming and appropriation of those three things,
without reference to the Divine Principle within the heart
of man, without repentance for our sins, without any true
understanding of the meaning of our existence, is doing
to the very fabric of our world, so that time itself begins
to hurtle towards death? We set our minds, individually
and collectively, upon false goals. We look in the wrong
direction. Knowledge, ecstasy, and power become for us
ends in themselves; and in pursuing them we lose them,
for they belong not to us as we are in ourselves, but to
the nature of the angels of God. We have forfeited that
nature, and shall regain it only as we learn to hold time
back, pursuing our one true end in submission to a will
that is higher than our own. Our lives must be limited by
that will. As we submit to this limitation, its constraining
aspect will be lovingly removed, until we emerge into the
limitless freedom of the timeless present.

Knowledge, ecstasy, and power are a trinity linked

together in the practices of magic; and, on the highest level, in the sacraments of the Church. Bestowed by the Holy Spirit, they are wisdom, joy, and faith: wisdom in the things of God; joy at all times; faith to stand firm in all trials, and to accomplish whatever is required of us in accordance with God's will and providence. To receive these gifts of the Spirit is to be "in Christ." To be "in Christ" is to receive these gifts. Demanded and seized upon as a "right," they change out of all recognition. Like Faust, we receive them at the hands of fallen angels—the fallen angels of our own corrupted spiritual and intellectual powers; and they will cast us down as Lucifer was cast down, further than our minds can think or our bodies cling to life, into a world of total incoherence.

The study of metaphysics and theology has to be related, at all points, to our everyday experiences in this world. We have to be able to see how knowledge, ecstasy, and power, under the sign of Lucifer (as they stand today) relate to our science and technology, our educational theories, our sexual lives, the arts we practice, the entertainments we enjoy, the social structures we create. The sign of Lucifer is in the ascendant at the present time. Knowledge, ecstasy, and power have never before been sought by man with such bleak avidity and so total a disregard for the "one thing only" that transforms them into what originally they were meant to be—the gifts of God.

15

Knowledge or Wisdom?

Knowledge, insofar as it is separated from wisdom, is at best a cluttering up with superfluities of the mind, at worst an appalling danger—to the faith of the individual, to the purity of his actions, finally (and in similar ways) to the collectivity within which it is put to use. Knowledge, which is, essentially, the very purpose for which man was made (so that God might know Himself) can become the most effectual means of deflecting him from that purpose. Knowledge of "things" without God is the opposite of the knowledge of God and of "things" as they are in God.

The Church's traditional prohibition against magic arose on account of its being, by definition, the acquisition and putting to use of knowledge outside the limitations imposed by obedience, for the sake of power, whether or not the purpose of so doing appears at the time to be legitimate. The magician, no matter how benign may be his intentions, relies upon his own judgment to manipulate the secrets of nature on the psychical level, in the direction of his own self-chosen ends. The wise man, on the other

140

hand, submits himself, and the collectivity to which he belongs, to the universal laws of God, as these are interpreted by the tradition he serves and by the inspiration of the Spirit as this is received in the heart and communicated to the mind. For such a man, his personal judgment is reserved for "unimportant" things—until he learns the final lesson that there are no "unimportant" things, and that his every word and action must emerge from free submission to a higher will. Then, and only then, will he have the "right" to uncover the secrets of nature, and pass on his knowledge to those who have shown themselves worthy to receive it and put it to a proper use.

Unless the natural sciences are pursued under a discipline of conscious obedience to a higher power, they are a form of magic. Ideally, they should form the curriculum of a school within a school under the auspices of the Church or whatever religious institution is appropriate to the time and place. In a secular society such as our own, the attitude of mind adopted by the scientist towards his research, and the limitations he imposes upon himself, can be determined only by the voice of conscience. This is not to be understood as the individual's personal judgment. Conscience is the voice of the Spirit within the heart, and the faculty that listens to that voice. It is the interface between the soul and the Divine. From the point of view of the collectivity, however, the individual conscience of one man is not enough. Albert Einstein was a man of conscience. Unhappily, on account of the spiritual alienation of the collectivity, his work was used to forward the line of research that destroyed Hiroshima and may eventually destroy the planet Earth.

We have tried to define what it means, individually and collectively, to be "in Christ." Nothing could be more obviously and catastrophically removed from that state than the science and technology of the present time. One of the

more poignant ironies of the situation is that while we know
so very much more than is good for us, we do not know
nearly enough. Unlike our forefathers, whose activities were
circumscribed and directed by religious considerations, we
sneeringly neglect those higher sciences that might show
us some of the ways in which we are going wrong. We
do not pay attention to anything in the realm of nature
that cannot be contained within a physical experiment. Yet
nature is not really understandable until we perceive it as
having a psychical dimension which connects it, through
man, with the higher spiritual levels that ascend as far as
heaven itself. In the ancient world science was far wider
in its scope than it has become in the post-Renaissance
West. We no longer study the laws of synchronicity as
partially revealed in the motions of the planets, the function
of material substances as conductors of psychical and
spiritual energies, the power of sound and of certain
combinations of sounds, the influences exerted by the shape
and proportions of buildings and other artifacts, the forces
associated with particular sites. Our methods of healing are
crude when regarded from the point of view of the ends
taken for granted by societies that were based upon faith
in a life beyond death.[1] So we hurl ourselves into discovery
after physical discovery, without a glimmer of understanding
of the psychical and physical havoc being wrought by these
discoveries. And what if we did, at last, begin to
understand? . . . In a disorientated world, any general
increase in knowledge is an increase in peril. In the hands
of a secular society, the science of physics may be
horrendously abused, but the science of the soul could be
put to an infinitely more terrible use.

Knowledge must not be indiscriminately popularized;
neither should it remain so guarded as to be inaccessible
to those who are capable of using it, under God, for the
common good. Used in this way, it becomes a part of the

"one thing only" that Plato bids us seek. It becomes part of the means of our return. The idea of an esoteric knowledge carefully guarded by an elite few must be understood before it is prematurely judged. Except in cases where the "few" in question have been corrupted by power (which will happen insofar as they cease to be submissive to the promptings of the Spirit, who alone is the source of all power, and set themselves up as *possessors* of the knowledge that has passed to them in trust), there will always be a means for those who are spiritually qualified to receive a particular kind of instruction, to receive that instruction—and to receive it by degrees within an appropriate discipline. It is a part of the task of those who are the trustees of knowledge to be constantly on the alert for new students. Generosity in imparting wisdom is a characteristic of the wise. There are, however, two major perils attached to such a system. The first is the temptation of power on the part of the elite. The second is the demand for power on the part of those who are dissatisfied with the level of knowledge that is actually commensurate with the degree achieved in their spiritual and intellectual development. These two dangers feed into one another. Like any other pair of opposites in a dualized world, they confront and react upon each other until a point is reached when one or the other of them "wins" for a period of time, after which there is a "revolution" and the other comes uppermost. The history of Christianity in the West provides us with an only too obvious example of this process.

> Those who love the Truth in each thing are to be called
> lovers of wisdom and not lovers of opinion.
>   Plato, *The Republic*

Allied to the prohibition against demanding knowledge for which one is unqualified, is the scorn of "opinions" to be found embedded in the writings of saints and sages of every one of the great religious faiths. Contrary to the modern idea that a child should be encouraged to "think for itself" and produce its own little personal iconoclasms from the moment of learning to speak, religious tradition has no uses for "questions" that are not asked of necessity, in humility, from the motive of a longing for the truth. In the school of Pythagoras, where the higher Mysteries were approached by way of studies involving mathematics, music, astrology, natural methods of healing, and various exercises to promote a normal and balanced way of life, the probationer was required to listen for two years without opening his mouth! This two-year period was known as the degree of "Hearer." The whole period of probation lasted five years, after which there was a ceremony of admission to the brotherhood. The religious Orders of medieval Christendom were based upon the same principles, and the great universities were conceived as functions of the teaching authority of the Church.

The *Brihadaranyaka Upanishad* contains a delightful rebuke uttered by the sage Yajnavalkya when a Brahmin lady named Gargi persisted in questioning him:

> "O Gargi," replied Yajnavalkya, "do not ask so many questions lest your head fall off! You are asking too much about that divinity of whom we should not ask."
> Thereupon Gargi stepped down and held her peace.

However, the prohibition against asking too many questions presupposes that adequate teaching will be provided, and that answers will emerge if one has patience. Similarly, discouragement of "opinions" presupposes that there is another and a better way of forming judgments. Under normal conditions that way is by attention and obedience to a received wisdom, leading on to the knowledge of the heart. Under abnormal conditions, such as our own, without any reliable source of instruction other than books selected from a vast confusion of literature by oneself, the question arises of how one may distinguish between a firmly held "opinion" and a certain knowledge of objective truth. A belief can be passionately adhered to without of necessity being true. Nowadays we are all supposed to have "opinions," but to confess to a religious conviction is to be asked immediately, "How do you know? Why should your opinion be any better than that of someone else?" It is not an unreasonable question. In a society that is spiritually unhinged, every sort of psychological, psychical, and spiritual derangement is liable to find its expression in religion. Is it, then, always a sign of arrogance to face one's critics and say simply, without any suggestion of superiority or aggressiveness, "I know"? Rumi did not think so. He wrote:

Anyone in whose soul God shall put the touchstone,
he will distinguish certainty from doubt.

16

Ecstasy or Joy?

Ecstasy, insofar as it is separated from the love of God, is a blind participation in the agony of cosmic death. This Mystery is expressed, for those who are able to receive it, in the gospel accounts of the Passion of Christ; and (in its true meaning, when this has been uncovered from beneath the literalistic and legalistic formulas that have been imposed upon it) in the Church's teaching about sex.

Ecstasy is known to our human nature in the mode of sexuality and in the mode of freedom. It is known also as creative activity and achievement. In the state of ecstasy we believe ourselves to be "as gods."

Human sexuality quivers upon the self-same point of intersection of the timeless with time as does the Cross of death. For every life that is generated upon earth, a death must eventually be given in exchange. This is a simple physical fact, but like everything else in the natural order, it points to something beyond itself. It points to the laws of balance and displacement. According to those laws, for every moment of ecstasy experienced in this world, there must be, somewhere in space and time, a moment of agonizing pain; for every orgasm of coming-to-be, there must be a spasm of death in the body of the coinherence. This is the result of the polarization of the opposites that was brought about by man. It is the reason that the Church, having exalted the sexual act to the level of a sacrament, also declares of it that it is (like any other sacrament) a participation in the heart of sin. The sexual act, which is sin insofar as it is the cause of pain and death, becomes a sacrament when it is raised up into the Cross. Again we are faced with the mystery of what it means to be "in Christ"—the awful distinction between what is and what is not that state.

In the matter of sexual relationships, the Church has first defined, and then literalized and legalized its own definition of the state of being "in Christ," sealing the intention of the partners with prescribed words and a formalized bond. In the true meaning of the marriage sacrament, the man and the woman, acting as their own priests, redeem the act of sex by directing it, through the Cross, into the consummation of the love of God. Their intention is required to be orientated towards that end, and to find expressin not only in physical sex, but in every action towards one another that is a part of their married life. The ceremony and the ring are formulas that the Church requires, as a safeguard against the sort of chaos in sexual relationships that has overtaken us at the present time. But a marriage may be formally correct without being spiritually "in Christ." Formulas are necessary *and* unnecessary, both at once. Without them, it would be impossible to sacramentalize the Mysteries; with them, there is always the danger of coming to believe that they *are* the sacramental reality itself.

A time comes when, if the formulas have become lifeless and inflexible, they break down. To prevent this from happening, it is necessary, from the first, to realize that they are not in themselves sacrosanct; and that in order to remain viable they must change, as every living thing must do, in response to the movements of the Spirit within a living Church. It is the state of inward identification with the inward reality behind the symbol of the Crucified and Risen Christ, not the ritual words and actions that have been prescribed in order to express that state within a particular historical context, that is binding and does not change and must be adhered to by faith. Outside that state, no moment of ecstasy, no aspiration to knowledge, no assumption of power, is legitimate. We accept death or we inflict it. Expressed in the mythological language of the Church, either we are crucified with Christ or we nail Him to the Cross.

The act of generation takes place upon that point where all times meet. It takes place at the instant in which the state of multiplicity comes into existence, and is itself the initiator of that state and the effectual cause of its continuance. It is the breaking up into the many of the One; at the same time, in identification with the Cross of Christ, it is the means of return of the many to the One across the barrier of death. The *Zohar* declares of the sexual act that it is, in every case, an invocation of the form of man, which form, as the divinely sealed and imprinted image of a human soul, hovers above the partners, awaiting its incarnation upon earth. (The Church's laws on the subject of birth control will never be understood — and therefore can never be satisfactorily reformed — until such profound ideas as this, which were originally the basis of those laws, are rediscovered in their pristine truth.)

The Church has both condemned human sexuality and exalted it, regarding it as being at the same time a perpetuation of the Fall, and an outward and visible sign of the union between the soul and God. We may have

some sympathy with the objection that neither of these
extremes involves the acceptance of sex as something natural
and beautiful in itself, unconnected with either mysticism
or sin. But this is to disregard the fact that our human nature
was created to transcend itself. In failing to rise above its
primal innocence, it degraded itself to the uttermost; so
that now, if we do for a moment recapture that innocence,
it almost instantaneously eludes us. In any case, it was not
given to us to hold. Blake called it the "wing'd life," to be
kissed as it flies; and we were intended to pass beyond it
to become the sons of God, in that state where there is
neither division nor generation, but the indivisible body
of the Christ.

These things are mysteries too deep for the Church
to attempt, exoterically, to explain. In relation to the laws
and formulations governing the whole complex of human
sexual activity, misunderstandings have proliferated and
hardened, both within the boundaries of the Christian faith
and among those who observe it from without. What is
urgently needed at the present time is for the Church, in
the persons of those who are in a position to make definitive
pronouncements, to return to the metaphysical principles
which originally shaped its now solidified and inappropriate
legislation; since it is only by returning to the roots that
radical reforms can legitimately be carried out. The
alternative is a choice between obstinancy and weakness,
or (as we are seeing at the moment) a bewildering mixture
of the two. Here, as elsewhere, the true way between the
opposites is not compromise, but a renewal of the
spirituality that leads us back to the primal revelation and
the meaning of the myth.

Historically and exoterically, the Church has exhibited
a tendency to treat the whole subject of sex on the level
of its physical manifestations, which in fact correspond to
a Mystery far higher and more all-embracing than can be

apprehended as a result of so limited an approach. On the
other hand, as we attempt to penetrate the veils of esoteric
Christianity, we find that only the Tantric modes of
Hinduism and Mahayana Buddhism have explored the
paradoxes of sexuality with a similar intensity, as being
central to an understanding of the human state. However,
where Tantrism has presented a spiritual discipline based
upon sexual exercises and an overt sexual symbolism,
Christianity has stressed the agony that counterbalances the
ecstasy, concealing the sexual aspect of its central Mystery
so effectually that it has, by this time, been forgotten by
the Church itself. In this matter, Tantrism and Christianity
are each other's opposite: the one invites the danger of falling
into obscenity and license, the other of retreating into
prurience, rigidity, and the kind of relentlessness that has
its roots in fear; yet both derive their teachings from the
same metaphysical source.

The god of ecstasy in ancient Greece was Dionysius.
Musician and charmer of animals, he represented a way
of reunification involving rapture-in-detachment, controlled
abandonment to the impulses of nature, the use of music,
incense, and the sacred dance. His worshippers, like those
of Siva, supreme divinity of Tantric Hinduism, engaged
in wild festivities which included dancing, wine-drinking,
and sex, the purpose of which was to awaken the spiritual
energies believed to be situated at the base of the spine,
and unite them with the Spirit of the god. Ecstatic hymns
and prayers invoked the divine descent. There are hints
in the apocryphal scriptures that early Christian ceremonies
followed similar patterns but with a far greater degree of
restraint. An extracanonical account of the Last Supper
describes how, when the meal was finished, Christ and the
eleven remaining disciples danced in a ring, singing a
mysterious hymn with repetitive responses like a children's
game (in the gospel version this is reduced to "and when

they had sung an hymn"). In another verison of the same
event, the youthful St. John (traditionally the only one of
the disciples who was beardless) reclines on the bosom of
the Master in exactly the same way as an adolescent youth
would recline on the same couch as his teacher, being fed
and caressed by him, at certain of the ancient ritual feasts.
In the latter case there was clearly a homosexual significance.
The Christian parallel would have a similar meaning, with
a spiritual rather than a physical emphasis.

The contrast between the two ways is nowhere better
illustrated than by the two methods developed respectively
by Christianity and the Tantric-Dionysian traditions for
the achievement of a higher consciousness by means of the
transformation of the energies associated with physical sex.
Where the Tantric sages devised exercises involving almost
incredible feats of self-control in the performance of the
sexual act, Christian mystics have eschewed such dangers,
advocating total abstinence—not as a rejection of sex, but
to bring about its metamorphosis into that of which its
physical manifestations are but the signature in terms of
our earthly life.

There are, however, lines of experiment within the
Christian tradition which resemble in their aims and
methods what is known as the "Tantra of the Right Hand
Path"—that is to say, those forms of Tantrism that are truly
orientated towards the One, and do not involve the
practitioner in any kind of self-indulgence. The cult of
controlled ecstasy based upon the Mystery of sex was
practiced by the early Gnostics, and later by the
troubadours, and the circle known as the *Fedeli d'amore*,
of whom Dante was the great exponent. Christian
practitioners were in search of the paradoxical state of
ecstasy-in-chastity by means of such exercises as lying in
close proximity to the loved one with a drawn sword placed
symbolically between. Meanwhile, in various magic circles

sexual energies were being utilized according to the same principles but in a very different spirit. Magicians, if they retain any vestige of Christian allegiance, do so only on the surface. They are concerned, unlawfully, with power, all the way down the scale from the "white" magic that is used—or at least intended to be used—for beneficent ends, to the most degraded forms of the "black art" involving hideous rites.

The death of Dante's Beatrice appears in his poetry as a mode of the Dark Night of the Soul in which all images are temporarily lost. Unlike St. John of the Cross, who sought for the soul's Beloved in darkness, Dante recovers the image and cultivates it as a transparent focus of contemplation, until it merges into that of the Virgin at the center of the Mystic Rose, symbol of the heavenly coinherence. The poet's progress in love exemplifies the Christian way of transcending not only the physical but the psychical ecstasy of sex, in order to achieve the higher levels of interior prayer and ultimately the beatific ecstasy itself. Rumi, Ibn Arabi, and others among the great Sufi mystics, followed the same path. For them, as for Dante, ecstasy was for God only. The "friend" of whom they wrote in rapturous adoration was an image concealing, yet revealing, that which lies beyond all images. If their language was misunderstood by the many who were not yet so far advanced along the path of heavenly love, they asked only that it should be understood by those who had shared the same experience.

This mystical ecstasy which is, for the Christian, the reward of his pilgrimage, the consummation of the time-process that has faithfully been traversed from the moment (symbolized in baptism) when his innermost intention was reorientated to its proper End, is described in the writings of the mystics as the kiss of God. Its first level of manifestation is the kiss exchanged between a man and a woman in perfect love. This is, traditionally, the origin of the earthly appearance of Sophia, the Virgin who will give birth to the Christ. Anna and Joachim, Mary's parents, exchange a kiss at the Golden Gate, which is the entry to Jerusalem, City of God, mode of the Holy Femininity, typifying the soul opened up to the inflowing and fertilizing Spirit. So, it is said, was the Virgin conceived, by divine intervention, in the womb of an old woman (that is to say, not in the natural order, but in a realm above that of nature, into which nature has been raised up).

This ecstasy is perfect freedom. It has soared above human desire, which is a bondage associated with death. In Buddhism, desire is declared to be that which binds the monadic consciousness to the Wheel of Time. Buddhist mysticism is a search for the state of perfect contemplation in detachment from the world, in which the enlightened sage presents himself as the example for all to imitate that all may receive enlightenment. Christian mysticism goes further. It speaks, as do the Sufis, of the pure desire for God, which is the higher form of *eros*, the spiritualization of sexuality in an act of total submission to God's love. Eros, in its physical aspect, directed away from its true course towards an illusory fulfillment, strains towards the infinite, seeking its consummation in a suicidal spasm of identification with the elusive image of a false beloved. It is Dante himself, supreme poet of the *Fedeli d'amore*, who shows us Paolo and Francesca imprisoned forever in the outermost circle of hell as a punishment for this sin—of which the most terrifying example in mythology is the swooning anguish of Tristram and Isolde, whose love is the result merely of a "potion," illusory as the dreams brought about by Shakespeare's mischievous Puck playing tricks upon poor humans in the wood of dreams. No state of bondage could be more complete than this. And yet there is a sense of freedom in unlimited passion, just as there is an experience of ecstasy in the act of throwing off all social and psychological constraints.

The sense of freedom is produced when pent-up energies are released. Cults of "freedom" (almost invariably associated with eroticism) involve the release of soul-forces that should never be set free until, as a result of long training and from a pure motive, they can be properly dealt with and transformed. In the Tantra of the "Left Hand Path," all forms of limitation are denied; initiates engage in orgiastic rites characterized by frenzied dancing, psychical manifestations, drunkenness, disorder, and dirt. The "Right Hand Path" is that of Wisdom; its principle is that of the gradual freeing and controlling of the psychical powers, its symbol, the god who first sets free and then subdues the demons of the lower realms. The Christian method is less obviously dangerous, while involving special dangers of another sort. Where the Tantric practitioner strives to achieve control-in-freedom by releasing his psychical nature to the uttermost and then, as it were, seizing it bodily and holding it in check, the Christian mystic practices asceticism until, like St. Antony in the desert, his "demons" release themselves and he must suffer their assaults. Paintings of St. Antony being all but smothered by his "demons" remind us of the fearful risks incurred by those who, unlike the saint, inflict upon themselves harsher mortifications than they are spiritually qualified to undertake. St. Antony, it must be assumed, was able eventually to subdue and transform the dark forces within himself. Those who are not yet able to achieve this (because they lack the simplicity and the faith) should be wary of the kind of practices that release demonic entities into the environment. The religious Orders have been, traditionally, aware of these dangers, and have dealt with them firmly under the Rule of Obedience. Enclosed convents, in particular, can rapidly become sources of miasmic pollution spreading beyond their walls, if the Rule slackens and the correct method of interior contemplation ceases to be understood. The Lord Himself, because the hour had not yet come when he would take all negative things and transform them in his own sacrificial death, compelled a horde of demons to enter into a herd of swine. "Poor swine!" we say too easily; but the story is there to show us how "before" the Cross there is no way of dealing with evil that does not drive it to some other place.

"Love God," Augustine said, "and do as you like." To love God is perfect freedom. But what does it mean to love God? Few, if any, of us really know. The late Father Vincent McNabb chose for the inscription above his grave the words spoken by St. Peter, in an unfamiliar but allowable translation: "Lord, thou knowest *if* I love thee." No one should dare to say more – or less. The Church has called its faithful to a life of freedom-in-obedience in preparation for the state of truly loving God. Anyone who has stayed, for however short a time, in a properly regulated Religious House, will have had an opportunity to observe how its disciplines produce a rhythm corresponding to that of the seasons and the stars, and need never be felt as a constraint. This kind of obedience, practiced with skill and understanding, for a holy purpose, is a sure and safe way of entry into the perfect freedom of the saints. It produces, not (save in rare cases) ecstasy, but joy.

Joy is a higher and a deeper thing than happiness, and can exist where happiness is absent. It is possible to be intensely sad, and yet to be aware of joy. Joy is, or can be, a perpetual state; whereas simple happiness, although it is a good in itself, is not appropriate to every time and place. The Church, in its provision of holy days and feasts, has sanctified happiness and confirmed it as being a part of the life "in Christ," a lightness and sweetness as of sunshine that breaks through the clouds of sorrow that enfold our world. Happiness, in a world of pain, cannot be more than a recurring interval for those who have compassion in their hearts. But we are not permitted to despise it. Those who do so are not Christians; they are the sorry victims of a secularized society who have forgotten what happiness is, because power, money, and the unlimited widening of "experience" have been put in its place. In such a society the very nature of human happiness (which mostly consists in things that are becoming less and less available to us, on account of the artificiality, restlessness, and violence of our way of life) gradually ceases to be understood.

It is written in the holy Qur'an: "Lo! The God-fearing are among gardens and watersprings."

That is joy. It is enough. Ecstasy has been granted in this world, to some, but by no means, all of the saints. It is one gift among many that may be given or withheld. We should leave it at that.

17

Power —
or Humility and Faith?

> And unto Adam [the Lord] said . . . cursed is the ground
> for thy sake; in sorrow shalt thou eat of it all the days
> of thy life. Thorns also and thistles shall it bring forth
> to thee; and thou shalt eat of the herb of the field. In
> the sweat of thy face shalt thou eat bread, till thou return
> unto the ground; for out of it wast thou taken: for dust
> thou art and unto dust shalt thou return.
>
> Genesis

It is often mistakenly supposed that the "curse of Adam"
as recorded in the book of Genesis is intended to reduce
sinful man to a state of permanent enslavement. It seems
to say that Adam's sin has set nature in opposition to him
and to his children to the end of time. "Thorns and thistles"
shall be his lot in life; and in death he shall have no hope
save that of returning to the hostile ground. From the point
of view of the Church, which uses this story as an integral
part of its myth, this is true only of mankind in the state
of being left to itself. Aligned to the Body of Christ, Adam
emerges from this state to receive the sonship that was not

yet his, even in the state of Edenic innocence "before" his
primal sin. So in "this world" we participate in the two
conditions: that of Adam's sin, which brought about his
fate of toil and pain and death, and that of his eternal life
in Christ. From the one to the other we return. And as
we do so, the curse is lifted and becomes the Cross. From
the Cross there is no escape, but it is itself the means of
our release.

We advance against the grain of a curse, drawn forward
by an infinite attraction and, as we yield to that attraction,
the assistance of a divine and invincible Power. The two
infinities draw away from one another, and our world is
poised, balanced, held in a tension, between the two. Our
actions and undertakings will always face either towards
God through the Cross, or downwards into the vortex of
our own self-chosen, self-inflicted death. In both cases we
are powerless of ourselves. In the former we receive power
from above and are sensible that it is not our own. In the
latter we experience, for a time, the illusion of being
powerful on our own; and when, as must inevitably happen,
the curse overtakes us, we may either begin to understand,
or we may rage against our fate and be guilty of what were
previously unimaginable sins. Our fallen "powers" then
become as fallen angels, tempting us to anger, greed, lust,
and all the wickedness that would cast us into hell if no
higher power intervened on our behalf and enabled us, even
at the last moment, to repent. This is a picture of our earthly
life. Corporately and individually, we had better understand
it. It is not "merely" a question of metaphysics. It is a
question of every single thing we say or do, from the way
we harness nuclear power to the way we shut a door or
kiss a child or cook lunch.

We are said to be entering into a new age, under the
sign of Aquarius. Many people like to believe that this new
phase of history will be marked by a raising of the level

of human consciousness and the acquisition by humanity as a whole of spiritual and psychic powers such as were previously limited to a tiny minority of exceptionally favored individuals. An astonishing number of cult associations, some even calling themselves "schools," loosely connected with Sufism, Buddhism, Hinduism, theosophy, spiritualism, psychism, magic, even, in at least one instance, all these and more in a single mix, endeavor to reassure us that our present troubles are but the birth pangs of this happy state. The fact that not one of the great world faiths has promised us anything of the sort, but the exact opposite, appears to have passed unnoticed. How, then, should we explain this optimism?

It is true that the sign of Aquarius stands for a new stage in human life. What is easily forgotten is that we distort our own destiny by the actions that repeat again and again our primal sin. What actually happens and what "should" or "might" have happened are very different; but there is always a connection between the two, in the sense that the tendencies discernible "in our stars" reflect a plan we have defied. Astrology, as practiced in the ancient world, was the science of what Carl Jung called "synchronicity." It traced a divinely laid-down pattern in the skies, and showed how an understanding of that pattern assists us in tracing the unfoldment of human destiny here on earth. Our distortion of that destiny produces travesties of the great designs that dance and sing and swing above us in the depths of space. So now, when we "might," under God, have been spiritually prepared to use the latent psychic energies that are present in the earth and in ourselves, to perform extraordinary feats of communication, healing, travel, and the general betterment of human life, we have chosen instead to develop an unnatural and uncontrollable technology which tempts us with illusions of power while it sweeps us, like lemmings, towards self-inflicted misery and suicidal forms of death. Power is in the hands of God. Even that illegitimate power that we seize for ourselves and then misuse is of God and cannot be taken from Him; without his permission it could not be harnessed, any more than, without his permission, I could lift my hand to my face. What we are doing is to snatch what is not our own, transforming it as we do so into images of our own defiance.

In a secularized society, social and political structures divide themselves brutally into "left" and "right," with an indeterminate area generally described inaccurately as "democracy" hovering in between, in a perpetual swing from reaction to compensatory reaction without hope of either stability or creative change. Traditional societies, on the other hand, for all the faults and abuses that are inevitably introduced into their structures in the course of time, are regulated in accordance with the laws of God as interpreted by the founders of their respective faiths. Those structures should never be abandoned because they have been abused, unless they have become so degraded by abuse that a balance has been irrecoverably upset, and the living Spirit is no longer present. In the latter case it will be necessary to return to the principial ideas behind the forms in question, and await the appointed time to create for them a new unfoldment. For instance, the principle of equality-in-inequality—that is to say, equality of persons in conjunction with inequality of function and the status associated with function—can take many forms, and if necessary, the forms may change, but the principle itself is indispensable for the proper ordering of society in the bonds of time. Power descends from the higher levels of being to the lower, flowing through an ever expanding number of individuals, by means of providentially arranged structures accepted by those for whose situation they have been designed, because they have been established by a tradition believed to have been ratified by divine assent.

Without those structures, and that acceptance, there is nothing left to us (whatever illusions we may temporarily cherish) except to labor under Adam's curse.

That is the meaning of tradition in its social aspect. Where the meaning has been forgotten and the system abused, this is almost always the result of a power lust, manifesting first at the top and then, in reaction, at the bottom of the social scale, causing the structures of society to harden and eventually to be destroyed. Power claimed by a class, or an individual, or vaguely on behalf of a "majority" (which is a meaningless concept to which nothing in reality corresponds) is a power usurped from God. Before God every human being is a servant, and God will raise up every human being to receive the privileges of a son. This does not mean that there is a total absence of "inequality" in heaven. (Dante makes it clear, in his great poem, that there are grades of blessedness in eternity.) It means that the heavenly "inequalities" are not, by definition, such as can be a source of envy or of discontent. Meanwhile, the inequalities of function, and of the status belonging to function in "this world," indicate no essential differentiation, but the providential apportioning, in the temporal order, of tasks to be performed. In the unimaginable context of "all times" each one of us may (as God wills) be called upon to undertake all, or many, or only one of the countless tasks that are needed for the preservation of our world until the end of time. Because these tasks have a symbolical aspect that is both valid in itself and necessary for the proper exercise of authority under God, this-worldly honors are attached to them in varying degrees. If we would understand these things, instead of misinterpreting them disastrously on account of the abuses of power that have poisoned the course of history, giving rise to reactions that have proved to be no less horrible in their results, we should study the words of the mystics. And we should do so in a spirit of

detachment from the political and social turmoils of a world
that has forgotten what it means to live in harmony with
heaven.

> Each knows his allotted grade and seeks it as a child
> seeks its mother's breast, and iron the lodestone. To
> occupy or even to aspire to a higher grade is impossible.
> In the grade in which he is placed each sees the
> realization of his highest hopes. He loves his own grade
> passionately and cannot conceive that a higher could
> exist. If it were not so, heaven would not be heaven
> but a mansion of grief and bitter disillusion. Nevertheless,
> those in the superior, participate in the enjoyment of
> the lower grades.
>
> Ibn 'Arabi

Dante is addressed by a blessed soul in the outermost
circle of Paradise:

> Brother, the quality of love stilleth our will, and maketh
> us long only for what we have, and giveth us no other
> thirst. Did we desire to be more highly placed, our
> longings were discordant from His will who assigns us
> to this place. But that, as thou wilt see, is not able to
> happen in these circles, since here of necessity love rules.
> And when thou dost rightly consider its nature, so wilt
> thou understand how it is of the essence of beatitude
> to exist in harmony with the divine will.
>
> Dante, *Paradiso* III.70

The above passages refer to a condition which is neither
our final End—declared by the mystics to be deification
in Christ—nor a mode of being that we are capable of
experiencing fully in this earthly life. Our pilgrimage in time
is the process of real-izing the state that Dante and Ibn 'Arabi
describe. Insofar as we do so, we find ourselves "on earth

as it is in heaven." In time, we "change places." He who is a king today was yesterday, or will be tomorrow, a slave—if not in the same lifetime, then in another. When we read in the holy Qur'an that "there is not one of us but has his known station," this is a reference to the place assigned to each one of us in the heaven of rest which is the metamorphosis of this earth. It also refers to the fact that here, on this earth, given the fidelity of society to the laws of God, everyone is given sufficient indication of the tasks he is intended to perform. In time, he may "change places," but here and now he can be at rest because he knows, at all times and in all places, what he is being called upon to do.

Simone Weil wrote, "If I had my eternal salvation placed in front of me on this table, and if I only had to stretch out my hand to take it, I would not put out my hand so long as I had not received the order to do so. At least that is what I like to think. And if instead of my own it were the eternal salvation of all human beings, past, present, and to come, I know I ought to do the same thing." ("In that case," she adds, with the humorless simplicity that in her is so touching and so exasperating, "I should mind very much.") Elsewhere she explains how such "orders" may be known. They come, she says, in the form of "everything which appears clearly to be a duty," and as "the compulsion of God's pressure," which she associates with the idea of a special vocation. "The most beautiful life possible has always seemed to me to be one where everything is determined either by the pressure of circumstances or by impulses such as I have just mentioned and where there is never any room for choice."

This is another way of expressing the idea, common to all the great traditions, that there are two sorts of "calling," and that everyone should follow the first unless and until he receives the second. The first is composed of the duties

of that "state of life" in which he finds himself as a result
of the so-called "accident" of birth (which is in reality no
"accident"). The second is the insistent voice of the Spirit
within the heart that calls a man away from his ordinary
occupations to a higher way of life—as a priest or religious,
or to carry out some special task. In a society that has
become secularized to the extent of no longer being situated
in anything resembling a traditional context, enormous
difficulties impede the application of these principles, which
are nevertheless basic to human existence. Few, if any, of
us nowadays are born into a situation which dictates specific
duties or defines for us a particular line of work. As for
the second type of "calling," not only is its validity denied
(modern churchmen, for instance, fall over themselves to
reassure us that there is no peculiar dignity attached to the
calling of a priest), but the unavoidable circumstances of
our daily lives, the chaos and the battle in the midst of
which we are compelled to live, deprive us of that silence
within which it becomes possible to listen to the inner voice.

In the *Bhagavad Gita* Krishna warns Arjuna: "O son
of Kunti, one should not relinquish the duty to which he
is born, though it is defective, for all undertakings are
surrounded by evil as fire by smoke."

The reference here is to Arjuna's unwillingness to go
into battle against his own relatives. Th Lord Krishna is
playing the part of his charioteer, at the same time
explaining to him that his scruples are inappropriate to his
vocation as a noble warrior. To fight is "the duty of thy
calling" in a defective world where fighting inevitably takes
place. The whole of this marvelous poem is a dissertation
on the meaning of action, in which it is made clear that
the motive behind all our works must be obedience, without
care for the result: "Let the motive be in the deed and not
in the event." When this is remembered there can be no
harm, for all things are beneath the hand of God.

"Wherefore, perform thou that which thou hast to do, at all times, unmindful of the event; for the man who doeth that which he hath to do, without affection, obtaineth the Supreme." Julian of Norwich clarifies the matter further by explaining that "sin is no deed"; from which statement she proceeds to the idea that all action is, in reality, performed in us by God Himself. "There is no do-er but He." Insofar as we make ourselves his instruments, He acts in us; and we were created that He might so act. This is the secret of the power that is wielded by the saint.

This basic paradox of nonaction in action, in which God's action takes over our passivity, so that we ourselves begin to act in Him, is clearly illustrated in the disciplines and customs of the religious life, which came into being as a sure way of remaining open to what Socrates called "the intimations of the will of God." Nominally, at the time of writing, the religious orders within the Church survive, although in an increasingly secularized and (from the point of view of anyone who knew them even twenty years ago) unrecognizable state. In this state they cannot fulfill their original function, or justify their continued existence. To study the meaning of a life dedicated to the three vows of poverty, chastity, and obedience under the discipline of a monastic rule, one must either rely upon books or seek out some isolated community (more likely to be Anglican than Roman Catholic) that has succeeded somehow in remaining untouched by change. We must study it, one way or another, if we are ever to understand the Christian metaphysic of action, prayer, and work.

The Rule of St. Benedict, upon which the entire edifice of Christian monasticism, with all its variations, was to be erected in the course of time, is the putting into everyday practice of the belief that an action is "no-deed" unless it is performed in us by God. At the time of the Second Vatican Council, there were still in existence a great number of religious houses, Anglican and Roman Catholic, where this idea was still recognized as forming the basis of training in the novitiate. This training involved not only the more obvious aspects of spirituality, but certain disciplines, the purposes of which remained obscure until the novice began, in daily practice, to work them out. They had the effect of teaching metaphysical truths at the same time as they conformed the individual to those truths. We may call them, for the sake of convenience, the discipline of order, the discipline of function, and the discipline of movement.

The discipline of order is (or was) the most immediately observable peculiarity of conventual life. It affects every detail of that life. It divides the times of day and night into phases occurring in a regular rhythm marked by the sounding of a bell, at which signal members of the community must pass, without an instant's pause, from one occupation to the next. The "when" and the "where" of every activity is prescribed. As there is a time for all things, so there is a place, not only for all things (which is also true) but for each and every embodied soul within the walls of a religious house. This discipline of placement is never allowed to be forgotten or relaxed. From the moment of being received as a postulant, each individual nun or monk receives a place in the hierarchical order which will only be changed in the event of its occupant being directed to some high office such as that of novice master, prior, or abbot. Apart from these offices, seniority is determined by the date of entrance. Thus when two individuals find themselves approaching the same doorway, no question arises as to who shall "yield the pass." (And yielded it must be; there is no question about that.) Another result of this discipline is that neighbors in seniority will be neighbors in refectory and choir, in physical fact, from the beginning to the end of their years in religion. (This circumstance, of course, one or both of them may not like at all; it then becomes a minor "mortification.") All of this is but the outward and visible sign of a grace that is bestowed upon every human soul who is born into this world, the grace of being uniquely placed within the Divine Order by Divine Provide-ence. For the true religious, who understands, whether intellectually or in wordless simplicity, the significance of the three vows, the outward placing is accepted as part of a covenant between the soul and God. The earthly order is seen as the sign or symbol of the heavenly state. This is so whatever may be its deficiencies; just as the decisions of the Superior are seen as representing the will of God, regardless of any human errors they may contain (always with the qualification that they contain nothing which involves the commission of a sin). Obedience is to that will as it is mediated downwards and outwards from one to another of a community held together by faith in the validity of its pact with God in Christ. Without that pact there is, of course, nothing left but tyranny and subservience with its inevitable reaction in revolt.

Monasticism came into being because the Christian community as a whole had grown lax in the traditions of the saints. Its rules and customs are a reminder to us all of what it means to follow a sanctified way of life. Thus the discipline of function, as this is practiced in a religious house, is intended to be an example to society, an ideal instance of a method that, with suitable adaptations, is universally appropriate. Behind it is the idea that since all work is performed for God only, it is unnecessary to consider (in the sense of being emotionally concerned with) either its outcome or its aspect of "self-fulfillment." In general, in the Christian monastic tradition, there has been a strong emphasis upon the virtues of practicality and common sense.

It is assumed that we should make use of these gifts: what is not assumed is that Divine Wisdom, of necessity,

intends things to "come right." The individual is presented
with a task which—certainly in religion, ideally also in "the
world"—has not been chosen by himself. He performs that
task. It is an aspect of the life of prayer; the actions it
necessitates are absorbed into prayer. Therefore, they are
performed as skillfully as possible, swiftly, but not hurriedly,
economically, but skimping on nothing. The results do not
matter. The destruction of the whole world, if God permits
this to happen, does not matter, because the reality of the
world cannot be destroyed; the reality of the world is in
God. A rule is imposed that only in the most exceptional
circumstances may one person offer to do another's work.
(This idea is echoed in the *Gita*: "Better is one's own duty,
although imperfect, than that of another well performed.")
In a convent such eventualities as illness and accident are
dealt with by authority, no one else being permitted to
intervene unless, in an emergency, the necessity for doing
so is made obvious by charity and common sense. "Mind
your own business" is a basic precept of the religious life.
Perform the action that is yours to perform, in obedience,
in simplicity, asking nothing for yourself—no credit, no
"fulfillment," no assurance of success.

The discipline of movement consists in becoming
aware, through a single-pointed concentration of the mind,
of every movement of the body down to the least change
of direction of the eyes or slightest gesture of the hand.
How a door is to be closed, how a slice of bread is to be
cut; from those actions involving skills that are hard to learn,
to those which for most of us are so nearly involuntary
as to pass unnoticed, the novice will be shown how each
movement can be made with economy and skill, without
clumsiness or fuss, and as nearly as possible in silence. This
discipline has to do with a teaching to be found in all the
great traditions, made visible in the sacred iconography of
them all, concerning what is called in Sanskrit *Mudra*, the

sacred poses and gestures that symbolize eternal truths. As all beings derive their meaning from the Christ, all language from the Word, so is all gesture made significant in relation to one central pose: for the Hindu, Siva dancing; for the Buddhist, the Blessed One's gesture of compassion; for the Christian, the outstretched arms of Christ Crucified and Christ Triumphant. On a less esoteric level, the rigorous yet gentle control of movement reflects the three vows of the religious life. By reducing self-expression to a minimum, it represents poverty; in its essential purity and simplicity, chastity; and as a form of continuous attention to the will of God, obedience. As an outcome of this discipline, there begins to be an integration of all the faculties, until the whole being, spiritual, mental, and physical, is involved in every action, small or great. As the great dancer directs his or her entire body from a central coordinating axis, so does the nun, but involving a higher center as directing agent, recollecting herself in all her acts. The word *recollection* was, until a very short time ago, one of the most familiar and often used in the vocabulary of the religious life.

Not everyone is called apart to become a nun or monk. But there is no single soul who is not called to follow the "one thing only" in poverty, chastity, and obedience of heart, as surely "in the world" as within the walls of a monastery or convent. The point of the monastic life consists in this: it makes the path more straight; no less painful, no less hard, but easier in a certain sense. The religious rule is a constant reminder that all that is merely human in our actions (good actions and bad, it makes no difference) will ultimately be consumed. In tenth-century Egypt a wandering dervish named Niffari wrote:

> He stayed me in Death, and I saw the acts, every one
> of them, to be evil. And I saw Fear holding sway over
> Hope; and I saw Riches turned to fire and cleaving to

the fire; and I saw Poverty an adversary adducing proofs; and I saw everything, that it had no power over any other thing; and I saw this world to be a delusion, and I saw the heavens to be a deception. And I cried out, "O Knowledge!" and it answered me not. Then I cried out, "O Gnosis!" and it answered me not. And I saw everything, that it had deserted me, and I saw every created thing, that it had fled from me; and I remained alone. And the act came to me, and I saw in it secret imagination, and the secret part was that which persisted; and naught availed me, save the Mercy of my Lord. And he said to me, "Where is thy knowledge?" And I saw the Fire. And he said to me, "Where is thy act?" And I saw the Fire. And he said to me, "Where is thy gnosis?" And I saw the Fire. And he unveiled for me His Gnoses of Uniqueness, and the Fire died down. And He said to me, "I am thy Friend."

18

What Is Beauty?

The life dedicated to God has ever been dependent upon symbols as the means of its advance. This is the case because the whole of creation is a system of correspondences, level upon level, each expressing in its own terms the metaphysical reality which is the unchanging Form upon the pattern of which all lesser forms are built.

"The divinest and the highest of the things perceived by the eyes of the body or the mind are but the symbolic language of things, subordinate to Him who Himself transcendeth them all." Dionysius might have added that the same principle that applies to the divinest and the highest applies also to the lowest and the least. It is the unfailing similitude or correspondence of the things beneath to the things above that enables those with unworthy motives to "explain" the most sacred myths, rites, and symbols in terms of natural phenomena, thus destroying the dignity and meaning of the latter, which, in reality, exist only as reflections of their archetypes in the heavenly state. "As above, so below" is an ancient saying from the Orphic Mysteries, the sense of which is repeated again and again in the scriptures of East and West. In the *Zohar*, for instance: "God made this world in the image of the world above; thus all which is found above has its analogy below." And in the Aitareya Brahmana (VIII.2): "Yonder world is in the likeness of this world; this world is the likeness of that." One could fill volumes with citations from the scriptures and the mystics to the same effect.

Form comes into being through spirit. Therefore, since it is the breath of the Spirit of God that creates all the forms in existence, it follows that all the forms in existence express in their diverse ways the same Mystery of the image of God, which achieves its fullness in the Son of Man. St. Hildegaard, in one of her metaphysical visions, was granted a revelation which should help us to understand why the forms of earthly things cannot be other than analogues of the things above; since both are shaped by the same Spirit in the same likeness:

> I am the supreme and fiery force that sends forth all the sparks of life. . . I am that living and fiery essence of the divine substance that flows in the beauty of the fields. I shine in the water, I burn in the sun and the moon and the stars. Mine is that mysterious force of the invisible wind. I sustain the breath of all living. I breathe in the verdure and in the flowers. . . All these live because I am in them.

The Church's sacramental system, together with the liturgies and rituals surrounding it, and the buildings within which its celebrations take place, is built upon this idea of the correspondence between the Divine Order and the multitudinous phenomena of the natural world. The symbolic science of alchemy, which medieval Christianity learned from Islam and from esoteric Judaism, which was so closely associated with Islam, was able to express the journey of the soul towards God in terms of chemical processes, which effectually veiled the metaphysical meaning behind what appeared to be a merely physical operation involving material substances. Modern science dismisses alchemy as a kind of immature and fanciful chemistry; but modern science, which goes about its business by reduction, knows nothing of the symbolism of gold as the pure Light of Heaven, into which the soul of man will be transmuted in the crucible of pain. It was the anonymous author of the seventeenth-century alchemical treatise known as the *All-Wise Doorkeeper* who wrote:

> The Eternal Father of All Things, being not less wise in the ordering, than powerful in the creation, of the world, has made the whole universe to cohere by means of secret influences and mutual subjection and obedience, things below being analagous to things above, and *vice versa*; so that both ends of the world are nevertheless united by a real bond of natural cohesion.

In a properly functioning traditional society, there is a realization verbalized by the few but shared generally by all, of the identity between the earthly symbol and its heavenly archetype, whereby the symbol becomes, as it were, absorbed into the archetype, in which its reality consists. This realization is an absolute safeguard against idolatry on the one hand, and destructive iconoclasm on the other. St. Basil, in his *De Sanctu Spiritu*, tells us, "The respect that is paid to the image passes over to its archetype." This happens naturally where respect is of the right kind, because the archetype is the reality of the image. Rumi, in one of the most beautiful of his poems, makes a clear distinction between the symbol and its heavenly counterpart:

'Twas a fair orchard, full of trees and fruit
And vines and greenery. A Sufi there
Sat with eyes closed, his head upon his knee,
Sunk deep in meditation mystical.
"Why," asked another, "dost thou not behold
These Signs of God the Merciful displayed
Around thee, which He bids us contemplate?"
"The Signs," he answered, "I behold within;
Without is naught but symbols of the Signs."

    Elsewhere he warns against attachment to the earthly
form which passes away:

> Every form you see has its archetype in the placeless
> world;
> If the form perish, no matter, since its original is
> everlasting.
> Every fair shape you have seen, every deep saying you
> have heard,
> Be not cast down that it perished; for that is not so.
> Whereas the springhead is undying, its branch gives
> water continually;
> Since neither can cease, why are you lamenting?

    Jacob Boehme, that oddity among mystics, whose
revelations seem at times as if they are too great and blinding
for his simple mind to comprehend and express, gives us
this wonderful description of the making of a form after
the model of its archetype:

> A form is made in the resigned will according to the
> platform or model of eternity, as it was known in the
> glass of God's eternal wisdom before the times of this
> world.

    That is why this world is beautiful. An ugly or
meaningless object is one from which the true form has

partially withdrawn (if it had withdrawn altogether, the object could not be in existence) so as to produce a distortion of the sort that can only come about as a result of human interference. Natural death withdraws the form but without distortion: there is nothing ugly in death until human beings begin to fear it and unlawfully to bring it about by murder, suicide, and neglect. Beautiful forms appear in nature, and again in sacred art: painting, sculpture, poetry, music, and the dance. So man, as God's instrument, assists Him in the work of creation. All true art is sacred. At the highest level, its shapes, colors, and proportions are prescribed by tradition to reflect the heavenly archetypes. In nature the same harmonious forms predominate. The microcosm reflects the macrocosm, and midway between the two comes our earth in all the radiance of its God-given beauty, quivering in the precarious balance of the sundered attributes of its creator God.

Between earth and heaven rises the upward spiral of the spiritualization of materiality. From earth to the nethermost depths descends the vortex of the densification of spirit, and the psychical realm, which invisibly encircles mankind, participates in both. That is why psychical art, which can be marvelously beautiful, with its radiant colors and dreamlike images, is dangerous insofar as it does not submit to the disciplines of a religious tradition. Typical of this art was the Symbolist movement at the turn of the nineteenth into the twentieth century in England and France. William Blake and Samuel Palmer were precursors of this movement. The realms of dream and imagination can raise our spirits heavenwards to the level of paradise; they can communicate messages of prophetic warning; but their boundaries contain dreadful paths which will only be avoided (as Blake and Palmer avoided them) as the inward eye remains fixed upon a point above that of the soul's creative fantasies. The psychical realm has its own sky, its

own stars — and its own chasms of darkness. That is why
the artist who asserts his own autonomy has been popularly
identified with the outcast. Like everyone else, he is required
to practice obedience, but religious authority is likewise
required to make itself worthy to be obeyed. There is more
than one kind of artist, and for each one who functions
on the highest level of spirituality, producing works that
are anonymous expressions of the great metaphysical ideas
at the basis of a given tradition, there are many more today
whose works are less pure and less metaphysically accurate,
but are yet able to present us with images of beauty that
uplift us, through psychical envelopes, to the very verges
of the heavenly state. There is nowhere an exactly drawn
divide. Beauty is the touchstone of legitimacy; but we
should not mean by this that the artist is obliged to depict
only what is in itself beautiful. His sole obligation is to
lead us to a deeper understanding of the Mystery of Beauty,
not as the opposite of "ugliness" but as its redemption in
a moment of transcendence.

Plato declared, "By Beauty all created things become
beautiful." He meant by this that Beauty is an absolute;
it does not belong to beautiful things but has been bestowed
upon them, enabling them to exist by virtue of its presence.
(All things exist and are held together by the principle of
Beauty.) The Sufi Jami repeats the same idea: "Every beauty
and perfection manifested in the theatre of the various
grades of beings is a ray of His perfect beauty reflected
therein." And Dionysius: "The Super-Essential Beautiful is
called "Beauty" because of that quality which it imparts to
all things severally according to their nature, and because
It is the cause of the harmony and splendor in all things,
flashing forth upon them all, like light, the beautifying
communications of its originating ray . . ." "Beauty," he goes
on to say, "summons all things to Itself" and "draws all things
together in a state of mutual interpenetration." It has even

been said (notably by Ibn 'Arabi) that Beauty is higher than Love because it is the cause of Love. (Such statements are made in moments of ecstatic realization, and do not preclude the possibility of a seemingly "opposite" truth being affirmed at some future moment.)

From all this it follows that it is a sacred duty imposed upon mankind to cherish beauty—by creating it in the arts and crafts, by concentrating it in religious rites, above all by *seeing* it with undimmed eyes, and *hearing* it with ears attuned to a heavenly music; because, in accordance with a fearful justice, our world itself changes as we change. Beauty withdraws itself from the spiritually blind; and from those whose ears are deafened by discordant noise it retreats into the forgotten silence. The world is less beautiful now than it was once, not only because we are actively engaged in despoiling it, but because our common experience of it has changed. No longer do we see our earth "as it is in heaven." And so its very essence draws away from us, back into its own reality in the silence and the harmonies, the radiant colors and the vibrant peace of the paradisal state.

A religious rite is an invocation. Beauty calls to a greater Beauty. Like calls to like. The words used should remind us that words possess meaning only as they are grouped beautifully, in a proper order, around a central principle of meaning. (The need for a sacred language, which becomes the more pressing as the collectivity becomes increasingly alienated from its tradition, has this metaphysical basis.) One of the most dreadful mistakes that was made in the aftermath of Vatican II was the introduction of new liturgies and new translations of the Bible on the basis of the notion that beauty is of minor importance compared with universal "comprehensibility." The latter, as an aim possible of achievement, is in any case a chimera. A lifetime of dedication enables one to understand no more than the ABC of the Christian metaphysic, which cannot be reduced to a false "simplification" beyond a certain point without (as has, in fact, already happened) ceasing to make sense. Meanwhile, the traditional forms are so designed as to reach down to and raise up the understanding of each and every individual who participates in the rite, although his participation may consist in nothing more (but could there be anything more?) than staying still, an attentive witness to what is being done. Ritual, like art, should always be "above the heads" of everyone present, at the same time as it makes use of everyday things down to the earth beneath our feet. What it should never do is pander to the demands of a majority for what that majority imagines that it "likes" and "wants." Insofar as it does this, it becomes something other than itself. The expression of collective emotions on the human level cannot, by definition, be the same thing as the ritual expression of a metaphysical truth.

The architecture of a sacred building is an extension of the central rite that is intended to be performed within its walls; it aspires to the same sublime level and is an expression of the same faith; it is required to be beautiful. The new fashion of "house Masses" in living-rooms is not justified by the argument that the Mass is valid wherever it is celebrated, as this can be true only when the intention to celebrate it in an appropriate context is for some reason impossible to carry out. The essential purpose of the Mass is the uplifting of everyday life. If the intention, on the contrary, is to lower the Mass to the level of human understanding, divesting it of the attributes of beauty and majesty and simplicity (for a living-room, unless it happens to be a monastic cell, is no more likely to be simple than it is to be majestic), on the extraordinary grounds that, since nothing is ever to be regarded as "superior" to anything else, Chartres Cathedral itself is in no way superior to anybody's lounge, and no human soul has need to uplift itself to that which might sanctify and beautify it and raise it to a condition superior to that in which it finds itself at present —a question must arise as to the validity of what is being done. For what purpose is, in fact, being accomplished? There is all the difference in the world between the homeliness that can afford occasional informalities within a sacred context because that context *is* so fully and unquestionably sacred that it absorbs the informalities into itself without its equilibrium being upset (as when the Lamas in a Tibetan temple pause in their chanting to seat themselves on the floor and enjoy a cheerful session of butter tea)—and the coffee hours that are nowadays held in churches precisely for the purpose of demonstrating that a church is *not* a sacred place. We are the children of God; and we are permitted our moments of playfulness in His House, for just so long as we do not forget that it is His House. Even as we play, our thoughts should never be far from those of Jacob, as he stood at the foot of the ladder which leads upwards from the symbols to the heavenly archetypes and beyond, and cried aloud: "How dreadful is this place! This is none other but the house of God, and this is the gate of heaven."

19

What Is Worship?

To real-ize reality.

Ansari

It is often asked why, since our task is to real-ize the reality of this world, in all places and at all times, it is necessary to have sacraments (which are, by definition, moments of exceptional real-ization in particular places at particular times). This question ignores the fact that the process of real-ization itself involves a concentration and drawing together of the essences of earthly phenomena, by means of symbols, in the direction of their heavenly archetypes, and this same process, having reached a certain point, *becomes* a sacramental rite.

For the Christian, the whole world is seen as being drawn up, a partial reality, into the total Reality of the Sacred Host, before it can be lost in God. In one sense the outward sign must seem arbitrary: for the Buddhist one image, for the Christian another, for the Muslim a third. But this is not really the case. No symbol can be arbitrary which has appeared within the context of a living tradition, because in such a context human creativity and human choice function in obedience to the Spirit's breath. The Spirit is responsive to obedience. It withdraws itself as obedience is withdrawn; and as this begins to happen, chaos enters in; nothing stays properly related to any other thing, and what are still called "symbols" are better described as visual aids or ornaments. Words fall apart from one another, losing their meanings. Language becomes divisive insofar as it ceases to be integrated around a central religious concept finding expression in a single utterance (the Word carried on the breath of the Spirit). Then there are no more sacraments.

A sacrament is a particular kind of symbol or group of symbols designed to bring into manifestation the reality of its archetype. The Church has seven sacraments, six of which function as rays or aspects of the seventh, which is the Eucharistic sacrifice culminating in the Reality of the Sacred Host; while each one expands into and includes within itself the other six; the whole system being, from a Christian point of view, not only an image of, but a means of actually bringing about, an encounter between the world and God. (For "the world" read equally "the soul.") That encounter takes place whether or not we embody it in some specific form. But we need specific forms. They demonstrate the fact that the nearer we approach to the center, the purer, simpler, and more concentrated our activities become, until at last our very lives are drawn into the Eucharistic rite. The wine and the bread are symbols. But a symbol has no reality of itself; the wine and the bread are Christ's Body by virtue of having been wholly real-ized in Him. The Church has entered into a covenant with God that his Christ-Being shall be recognized and worshipped in a special way in them, and shall in them become a communication of eternal life. In this understanding the cup of wine is still a cup of wine; the piece of bread remains a piece of bread. If some magical operation took place, the entire meaning and purpose of the operation would be lost. But what is a piece of bread? Who and what are you and I, since nothing *is* in heaven or on earth save Christ-in-God and God-in-Christ?

The other sacraments are contained in the Eucharist. They remind us that, because we live in time, our life in Christ is broken up into stages, each one symbolized by a particular aspect of the central sacrament. There are six lesser sacraments because it is an ancient tradition that there are six spokes to the Wheel of Time, six ages of the world, six ages of man: birth, puberty, coming of age, maturity, old age, and death (Baptism, Confirmation, Order, Matrimony, Penance, and the Last Rites). To understand these connections we have to translate the idea of the merely physical and psychical lifeline into that of the Christ-life which follows the moment of spiritual rebirth. The Christ-line is thought of as being marked by successive experiences ("successive" because our minds oblige us to think in terms of linear time) which are, in reality, a single experience. The Eucharist is that single experience. From the moment of rebirth arises that of initiation by the Holy Spirit in the place of the heart; whence comes the stage of maturity-in-Christ, which makes of every man a priest, identified with his own archetype in the archetypal sacrifice; to be followed by the reunification of the "opposites" within the human soul, as its masculine and feminine elements reunite in the Mystery represented by the Nuptials of the Virgin in heaven. Thus marriage is, in a certain sense, the culmination of the lesser sacraments. Situated at the peak of man's experience in time, it symbolizes the fulfillment of his pilgrimage in time. Not for nothing were these words introduced into the Church of England marriage service: "O God, who has consecrated the state of Matrimony to such an excellent mystery, that in it is signified and represented the spiritual marriage and unity betwixt Christ and his Church. . ." Penance and the Last Anointing are the two sacraments belonging to the descending scale of man's earthly life. The one prepares him for death; the other dismisses him from this world. Thus the sacraments turn in a circle which we shall understand more readily if we think of it as beginning with Penance and passing through the Sacrament of Dismissal to that of the New Birth (for the circles of man's earthly life and of his life-in-Christ are as two waves that resemble one another but do not peak at the same moment). And let it never be forgotten that each one of the lesser sacraments leads directly into the Eucharist, in which all times are present.

The sacramental principle is absolutely basic to religion. The very word *religion* signifies a bond; and this is the essential meaning of a sacrament. The chosen form, by virtue of its own essentiality in heaven, represents a bond with heaven, regardless of the partial and imperfect nature of its timebound state. Thus the Dalai Lama *is*, for his Tibetan followers, the Presence of the Divine One, the Lord Chenrezig, in Tibet. He mediates that Presence, and is therefore known as *Kundun* ("the Presence"), a sacred function which in no way depends upon the personal character of the man himself. Islam circumambulates the Ka'bah as the still center of the worlds (as indeed it *is*, if we choose by a convention so to regard it), and venerates the Qur'an as the miraculously descended Word of God. No temporal imperfections may invalidate a pact with heaven that man has sealed by faith and wills to keep. A priest is no less a priest for being an evil man. The Host is no less God-with-us for being a scrap of sliced white bread from the supermarket.[1] The perfection of the Holy Qur'an remains intact, though one should point out some imperfection in the actual words that have been written

down. Validity is guaranteed by the intention of the
collectivity in question to encounter God in this way, at
this time, and in this place.

That word *intention* could almost be described as the
key to Roman Catholic mystical and sacramental theology
in the days before Vatican II. Its regular appearance in
numerous contexts was taken for granted by Catholics,
wordlessly understood by the simple, though not, it would
seem, by those "intellectuals" who were to be instrumental
in getting rid of it. Every Mass had its "intention." Familiar
prayers, such as the "Hail Mary," were said for various
"intentions." Congregations were exhorted to pray for the
"intentions" of the Pope. The idea behind this was closely
related to the Islamic emphasis on correct orientation, and
to Simone Weil's "It is the looking that saves us." The
motivating desire of the heart is the only true prayer: that
alone, no matter what thought may be formed with the
lips or in the mind, whatever one may think that one means,
is what one means before God. God sees only the intention.
The Pope's intentions, in his papal capacity as the
personification of the mind of the Church, are the Church's
prayers, those prayers that are central to the faith; above
all, the prayers of offering and of invocation which together
constitute the heart of the Eucharistic sacrifice. Lately there
has been so much uncertainty as to what is intended in
the sacraments, and the manner of their celebration has
been so ambiguous, that many Catholics are questioning
their validity and leaving the Church. For the Church *is*
its sacraments. They are its prayer; they are its acts; they
are its intercourse with God. Without the Eucharist there
is no Church in the sense in which the idea of the Church
has traditionally been understood.

Actions will be judged according to intentions.
Saying of the Prophet Muhammad

R. A. Nicholson, who translated the poems of Rumi, explains the matter from the Islamic point of view, as follows:

> As a rule, the ritual prayer is invalidated by facing in the wrong direction, but should the worshipper, owing to darkness or any other sufficient cause, fail to turn towards the Ka'bah, he does not lose the merit of his prayers, provided that he has endeavored to the best of his judgment and ability to ascertain the direction as accurately as possible.

The outward form is important but not all-important. All-important is the intention, which is proved by the care taken to carry out, down to the minutest detail, what is understood as being the will of God. When the forms themselves begin to fail, this does not matter, provided the intention does not fail. In darkness one orientates oneself towards the vanishing sacrament, the invisible Ka'bah; and that is enough. This, nowadays, is the situation of many who believe that the Church, as anything more than a society of good people concerned with social betterment according to the example of a personal, "historical" Jesus (bearing little resemblance to the figure described in the New Testament) is no longer in our midst.

The Blessed Sacrament is (as Simone Weil used to say, "by a convention") the is-ness of material things. The Host is the material substance of this world offered up to God to be transformed in Him. The wine is that same substance infused from above with the Spirit that turns "water" into "wine," the human baptism of John into that Fire from on high that is made available "in Christ." The two "kinds" are substantially the same; but the symbolism is of earthly rising in the one, of Divine descent in the other. The Eucharistic sacrifice is followed by the holy meal in which the communicant absorbs the Divine nature, which will then pervade his being and nourish him with the life that knows not death. Man eats God, not so as to be "as gods," but so as to be made God at the same moment as he is naughted in himself. There are a number of medieval paintings depicting a Tree divided down the central axis: on the one side it is the Tree of Eden, on the other the Tree of Life; from it Eve is plucking apples for the worldly, while Mary on the other side plucks and dispenses Hosts to the faithful who kneel at her feet. Eating has as important a place in the Christian Mysteries as does sex. To eat "in Christ," we must learn to cooperate in Him, husbanding the earth with reverence and sharing its fruits with justice, leaving none in want. Every meal should be an outward sign of fellowship in love. The Eucharistic meal, earthly symbol of the coinherence, betokens the instantaneous metamorphosis whereby the child of man becomes the Son of God.

But still the paradox remains. The sacraments, even the Eucharistic sacrament, are in themselves but outward signs. The saints were ever faithful to those signs. They loved them and rejoiced in them; yet Meister Eckhart and some others occasionally dare to indicate that the soul, at a certain point, no longer needs exterior forms:

> If I intend to cross the sea and want a ship, that is part and parcel of the wishing to be over, and having got to the other side, I do not need the ship.

And Rumi:

> . . .they that know the conventions are of one sort; they whose souls burn are of another. The religion of love is apart from all religion. The lovers of God have no religion but God alone.

The words of Jesus to the woman at the well are often quoted by those who would like to read into them what is not there, a license to dispense with the forms and customs of religion. Jesus himself appears to have been meticulous in observing all the practices that were expected of an orthodox Jew. He did, however, point out more than once that such practices were no more than a means to an end; and this, too, has been cited in evidence for what it clearly does not mean. To the woman at the well, when she tried to provoke him by drawing attention to the formal differences between the religion of the Samaritans and that of the Jews, he replied: "Woman, believe me, the hour cometh when ye shall neither in this mountain, nor yet at Jerusalem, worship the Father . . . God is a Spirit, and they that worship him must worship him in spirit and truth."

Perhaps we are living in that hour. It is hard to say whether Jesus was referring to the time when the outward forms will perish because, like Eckhart's ship, they have served their purpose, or to the evil days when mountain and temple alike will be despoiled, and we shall be tested as to whether we still possess the one thing needful for our worship. In the book of Revelation we are told that St. John in his vision of God's kingdom "saw no temple therein: for the Lord God Almighty and the Lamb are the temple of it." How many aeons of time must pass away before we shall be made worthy to dwell in that kingdom? And meanwhile . . .? The Mundaka Upanishad contains what is perhaps the purest and most beautiful of all scriptural exhortations to observe the rites, an outpouring of wisdom that falls upon the ear like the waters of the holy rivers which are India's sacraments:

The rituals,
      seen by the seers as the sacred verses,
      are variously explained in the three Vedas.

Perform them constantly,
    ye who desire truth,
    for they are your path to the world of the good.

When the sacred flame is kindled,
    and the flame is rising,
Offer with devotion between the sacred vessels.

If the sacrifice of fire is not followed
    by that of the new moon
    and that of the full moon,
    by that of the four months
    and that of the harvest;

If guests are not invited,
If offerings are not given,
    or given wrongly,
If the gods are not invoked,
The seven worlds stay closed...

Whoever performs the sacrifice correctly,
    when these seven are enlivened,
He is led by them,
    as the rays of the sun,
    to the world of the lord of the gods.

The radiant ones invite him,
    "Come! Come!"
    carrying him up on the rays of the sun.
They honor and glorify him, saying:
    "This is the holy world of Brahma,
    won by all your rituals."

But verily, these rituals are unsafe boats,
They cannot reach the farthest shore.
The Vedic sciences are but the lower
    knowledge.
The ignorant
    who take them as the higher,
    sink once more into old age and death...

The remainder of this sublime poem is a description of the supreme experience of union with the divinity that dwells beyond name and form.

Beyond all conception,
the one light shines forth.
It is the Great.
It is smaller than the smallest,
farther than the farthest,
nearer than the nearest.
The wise know it resting deep within...

As rivers flow into the sea,
losing their individuality
So the enlightened,
no longer bound by name and form,
merge with the Infinite...

And yet...

This knowledge may be taught
only to those who perform the rites,
only to those who are learned in the scripture,
only to those who with devotion surrender
themselves,
only to those who are established in Brahman.
To these alone and no one else.

20

What Is Prayer?

If we could but learn to pray, the answers to our perplexities (insofar as they need to be answered) and the knowledge of what we have to do, would be given to us, and all would become simple. But most of us do not know what prayer is.

Johanne Kelpius, of the School of Boehme, tells us what it is. "My prayer is my inclination, and my inclination is my prayer," he wrote. And that is all. If only it were not so difficult to believe. If only it were not so frightening. Because it means, clearly, that unless my heart is inclined towards God, I may spend hours on my knees, but I am not praying. On the other hand, it is a great consolation to reflect that vast numbers of people who say they do not believe in God are praying to Him in their hearts.

John of Cronstadt, a Russian Orthodox priest who died in the early years of this century, said simply, "Prayer is the breathing of the soul: prayer is our spiritual food and drink."

Putting the two definitions together, we see that we

must incline ourselves to breathe, eat, and drink spiritually, as ardently as we do physically when we find ourselves deprived of air and nourishment. (The sage Ramakrishna once held a disciple's head under water, and later told him that when he desired God as much as he had desired to breathe, he would be ready to receive the Divine vision.) It is not a question of kneeling down and saying things to God. Still less has it anything to do with the current fashion for pretentious exercises vaguely associated with the East. It is not even a question of saying the rosary or kneeling before the Blessed Sacrament. It is a question of desiring to be with God.

> Between me and thee is an "I am" that tormenteth me.
> Take by thine own I AM mine from between us.

In this prayer the Sufi mystic Al Hallaj defines the very first thing for which one has to pray. For until the "I am" is torn out, there is no way for anything else to get in. Even a ray of Divinity cannot pierce my "I am" until I ask, from my heart, that it should. And the asking of my heart must pierce through that same "I am" before it can get out.

A great deal of what is often called intercessory prayer operates in the psychical field, and would be more properly described as the creation of influences in that field. There is always this danger of confusing psychical, personal, and emotional experience with true prayer, which can never be anything but a turning towards God of the mind in the heart. Russian Orthodoxy speaks with a voice of ringing authority on the subject of prayer:

> The principal thing is to stand with the mind in the heart before God, and to go on standing before Him unceasingly day and night, until the end of life.

> Theophan the Recluse (1815-1894)

One of the most wonderful things ever said about
prayer is contained in the following sentence, part of a letter
written by Theophan to one of his penitents: "Try to
acquire a kind of soreness in your heart."

The subject of intercessory prayer is fraught with
difficulties because there are as many ways of "asking for
things" from God as there are levels of being from which
a request may originate. True prayer is the aspiration of
the higher part of the soul, where it merges with pure spirit,
uncontaminated by psychical entities belonging to the lower
levels of the personality. This aspiration calls down power
to be used only as God wills it to be used. Below this is
the kind of "prayer" which operates transpersonally by
means of intangible vibratory influences which may well
be those of sincere altruism and loving concern. Such
"prayer" can very frequently produce healings and other
beneficial effects, but it produces great dangers as well,
because it can slide over into magic as the human will begins
to manipulate events to produce a desired result. If we fully
grasped the necessity of adjusting a balance every time a
result is brought about, our prayers would become more
real, because we should never dare to pray for more than
we were willing to give.

The laws of balance, demanding a sacrificial operation
on the part of man-in-Christ for every evil that is banished
finally from this world, mean that whoever offers
intercessory prayer must accept that he himself may be
called upon to suffer the evil that he desires to eliminate.
This suffering may, indeed, not come to him at once, or
in a form that will have any obvious connection with his
prayer. The balance will be adjusted as God wills, but there
is no effectual intercession without sacrifice; that is the
meaning of the Eucharistic rite. At the other extreme, the
practitioner of magic, however well-intentioned, may
discover, when the truth of all his actions is revealed, that

he has implicated himself in things more dreadful than he knew. The practice of magic is one of the many factors that increase the population of a psychical realm known to *Kabbalah* as *Kallipot* or the "World of Shells," to the modern psychoanalyst as the negative contents of what he would call the unconscious mind. But modern psychology does not know the depths of this realm nor the extent of its horrors and how they come to be (if indeed they can be said to "come to be," for they do not in reality exist, despite the appalling effects that we enable them to produce). These "shells" of evil are the thought forms that the laws of balance bring about whenever a human soul exerts the personal will in opposition to the will of God. And every time we engage in illusory forms of "prayer," whether we are attempting to bring about some tangible result or simply indulging ourselves in "charismatic" experiences, we sink into the World of Shells, and emerge from it not only besmirched ourselves but exuding its influences on those we meet. Again, the great Orthodox masters of the art of prayer provide a clear analysis. They have given us the word *prelest*, which has the meaning of psychical or illusory prayer and the spiritual pride which lies at its roots. "For if a man," wrote St. Gregory of Sinai, "seeks God with obedience, questioning, and wise humility, he will always be protected from harm by the grace of Christ." The "questioning" here refers to the necessity of discriminating "by mental taste the gifts of the Holy Spirit from the fantasies and illusions of Satan." St. Gregory, in common with many another of the great spiritual masters, can provide no easy answer to the problem of making this distinction. He admits that the "illusions of Satan" may seem for a time exactly like a genuine experience of the grace of God. Obedience and a "wise humility" are the principles that will enable us to "taste" the difference.

Humility leads directly into what has been called the

Divine Darkness, which is not an absence of light but the antithesis of such an absence. Humility is the state in which the soul finds itself when it is withdrawn into the heart, expecting nothing, content to be silent and lost. Theophan makes it clear that we may come to this state gradually by the faithful use of "oral" prayer, which means chiefly "saying one's prayers" in the old-fashioned sense. The Orthodox make particular use of what is known as the "Jesus prayer," which is simply the repetition over and over again of the words "Jesus Christ, Son of God, have mercy upon me." The anonymous medieval treatise entitled *The Cloud of Unknowing* tells us: "Short prayer pierceth heaven . . . And why pierceth it heaven; this little short prayer of one syllable? Surely because it is prayed with a full spirit, in the height and in the depth, in the length and in the breadth of his spirit that prayeth it?"

For those who are drawn to the practice, saints and mystics from all the traditions have advocated the constant repetition of a sacred name. A Chinese Buddhist priest called Fa-chao declared, "When a man begins to call on the sacred name, a lotus flower begins to grow for him in paradise," which is, almost in so many words, what Rumi tells us in the poem which his English translator entitled "The Beauty of Death." "Everyone's death is of the same quality as himself" is the theme of this poem. It grows from a man's spirit like a leaf from a tree, ugly or beautiful as his soul has been ugly or beautiful.

> When praise of God has flown from his mouth,
> the Lord of the Daybreak fashions it
> into a fruit of Paradise.

21

What Is Certainty?

Who seeketh Me findeth Me
Who findeth Me knoweth Me
Who knoweth Me loveth Me
Who loveth Me I love
Whom I love I slay
Whom I slay I must requite
Whom I must requite Myself am the Requital.

These words, put into the mouth of God, are believed
to have been written by 'Ali, the son-in-law of the Prophet.
If they seem to represent an ideal of mystical devotion far
beyond the reach of more than a very few (among whom
few if any of us would dare to include ourselves), the truth
is that they must eventually apply to every one of us; since
every one of us, whether we will or not, is being sought
by God; and God does not give up the search.

Love that One Who, when you shall cease to be, will
not Himself cease to be, that you may become one who
will never cease to be.

Abu Sa'id ibn Abi 'l-Khayr (967-1049)

It is a false dream to imagine that there is some paradisal "afterlife" lasting forever and ever, in which we shall live as idealized versions of our present selves. If this notion is beginning to disappear in the general disapprearance of religious beliefs, that, at least, is no great loss.

> Everything that is thereon passes away;
> And there remains but the Face of thy Lord . . .
> Qur'an LV.26.27

We shall remain only insofar as we are willing, at last, to lose ourselves eternally in contemplation of that Face. For the mystics tell us that there is none other than God, and we had better believe them. Al-Hallaj writes of the spiritual pilgrimage of the Prophet Muhammed: "When he reached the Furthermost Limit he said: 'I cannot praise You as You should be praised.' When he reached the reality of the reality, he said: 'You are the only One who can praise Yourself.' "

This we know in theory; but we shall not know it as the heart knows the truth until we have allowed the shell of selfhood to be broken. And that breaking us, for most of us, aeons away in time; although if there is even now a hairline crack, it can be penetrated by the Spirit, who will not leave us after that.

All that we love is in God. When the journey is over, we shall see how this was so all the time, and that will be the last laugh.

> In the empty heart, void of self
> Can be heard the echoing cry
> "I am the Truth,"
> Thus is man one with the Eternal.
> Travelling, travel and traveller have become one.
> Shabistari

It is all perfectly simple. When all the scriptures and all the symbols and all the rituals and all the good marks and this, that, and the other are all burned up, all that matters will be all that is left. Fakhruddin 'Iraqui shall have the last word:

What is certainty?
God.

Notes

Chapter Two

1. If, as seems unlikely, this assumption were ever to be "disproved," it would not matter. The history that is amenable to being "proved" exists upon one timeline only. We do not have to worry unduly about it.

2. In this book references to "the Churches" and "the Church" apply generally to Rome, the Church of England, and the Orthodox Church. The idea of "the Church" as a man-made institution is misty at the edges: on the other hand, the sacred tradition passed on within the three Churches above mentioned remains clearly definable.

3. We are referring here to the mythical rather than the historical figure. The gospels make no distinction between this Jesus and the historical personality; and, since the historical personality was himself cast, by an overwhelming destiny, in a sacred role, there is, in many places, none to be made. Much confusion can, however, arise; and students of the New Testament should be constantly aware of the difficulties it presents in this respect.

4. The phrase "the transcendent unity of religions" was brought into use recently by Frithjof Schuon.

Chapter Four

1. Edinburgh University Press, 1981. I acknowledge my indebtedness to this chapter in Dr. Nasr's book upon which my exposition of the theme has, to a great extent, been based.

Chapter Six

1. In certain noncanonical scriptures associated with gnosticism, Adam and Eve are referred to as "the Adam" to emphasize their union-in-duality and the truth that each one of us contains and is contained within them both.

2. It is vitally important to distinguish between the essential teachings of a tradition, which will always possess their own principle of cohesion, holding them together in an inassailable integrity, and the surface interpretation dictated by men who have lost touch with the informing Spirit. The latter may do incalculable harm, but they do not affect the validity of the tradition itself as a vehicle of Truth.

3. "Hell" here does not mean the place of everlasting punishment. As in the Creed, the word is being used to denote the limbo in which departed souls await the coming of Christ.

Chapter Seven

1. Mary Magdalene "supposed him to be the gardener." Such asides as this, occurring in profoundly esoteric passages of scripture, should never be dismissed as insignificant.

2. The clause in the otherwise universally acceptable Christian creed, in which the Holy Ghost is defined as proceeding from the Father "and the Son."

3. To those who are unable to accept this differentiation, it has to be said that until the idea of the symbolic inequality of function is understood and welcomed as implying no insult or humiliation to anyone, but rather as producing a beauty and harmony in which all may rejoice, the ancient wisdom will remain a closed and inaccessible book.

4. This expresses in Christian terms a difficult concept, which we shall try gradually to elucidate.

Chapter Eight

1. Gary Zukav in *The Dancing Wu Li Masters* (Fontana/Collins, 1979).

2. *Ibid.*, p. 331.

Chapter Nine

1. An extraordinary series of twelfth-century graffiti to be found in various parts of Canterbury Cathedral repeats this theme again and again.

Chapter Ten

1. For the benefit of those who do not know, it should be explained that Islam venerates Jesus and Mary and the Mystery of the Annunciation, although its understanding and that of Christianity are somewhat different.

2. The prayer of Jesus in the Garden (Garden of Paradise, Garden of Olives,

Garden of the Resurrection) on the eve of his Passion, presents a mysterious paradox. He prays, "Not my will but Thine be done." Who, then, prays this prayer?

3. There are two hymns beginning with these words. The other is for Maundy Thursday.

4. In Persian: *gul* from the letters *gaf* and *lam.*

5. It must be understood that the teachings given here in connection with the two St. Johns are of an esoteric nature, and their exact sources cannot be given. These sources are concealed in the gospels and in numerous legends and apocryphal writings which must be studied deeply before their implications are revealed. In happier times than ours it was sufficient for such teachings to remain implicit in doctrines and practical instructions which were more easily understood. Nowadays when the very roots of Christianity are being undermined, it becomes necessary to make the estoricism more explicit.

Chapter Eleven

1. Tibetans regard the wheel as so fearful in its potential for good and evil that for centuries they forbade its secular use. The first wheels, other than prayer wheels, to appear in Tibet, were those of the thirteenth Dalai Lama's imported baby Austin car. This was acceptable because the Dalai Lama was a god, and was now revealed as having harnessed an exceptionally powerful demon.

2. It seems possible that this is less true in 1986 than it was in 1936. In the last fifty years world-time has been violently and unnaturally speeded up, while the lives of small children have been distorted by previously unimaginable forms of excitement.

3. The theory of eternal recurrence is dealt with extensively in the works of P.D. Ouspensky, Maurice Nicoll, and Rodney Collin. These three writers all belonged to the School of Gurdjieff, which tends to veer away from the central truths of the great religions by encouraging the idea of a "super-humanity" in what seems at times to be a Luciferian sense—although Rodney Collin was a Roman Catholic and a true mystic.

Chapter Thirteen

1. The expression "doing time" for the working out of a prison sentence is an example of how popular expressions often refer, in the oddest ways, to the truths of metaphysics.

Chapter Fourteen

1. Such as we are seeing today in the abandonment of the metaphysical dimension within the ecumenical movement.

2. An expression used by Simone Weil to denote the Divine Order made manifest in the created universe.

Chapter Fifteen

1. Superstitious methods of healing, such as were common, for instance, in medieval Europe, are crude in another way. When a traditional society lapses into superstition, this is generally the result of corruption at what should have been the seat of wisdom. In the Middle Ages, a corrupt priesthood resulted first in gross superstitons, later in the humanist reaction that was set in motion at the Renaissance.

Chapter Sixteen

1. We are witnessing, at the present time, an extraordinary resurgence of ideas and practices that are essentially magical rather than Christian or, in any sense, religious. In the Churches (Roman and Anglican) a sort of undigested Tantrism has become a potent influence. A morbid preoccupation with witchcraft is associated with certain apsects of the Women's Liberation Movement.

Chapter Eighteen

1. The sweet-tasting, cheap plonk that is nowadays often used for the Communion wine is an insult to God and man. This does not in itself invalidate the sacrament, although the disbelief implied by such indifference could arguably do so.